# *Historic Tales*
## *of*
# MANCHESTER
## CONNECTICUT

R OBERT  K ANEHL

THE
History
PRESS

Published by The History Press
Charleston, SC
www.historypress.com

*Front cover*: (*Top*) Horse-and-cart delivery was the height of efficiency for this North End Manchester market. *Courtesy of the Manchester Historical Society.* (*Bottom*) Looking north, or uptown, on Main Street in Manchester. *Postcard from the author's collection.*
*Back cover*: (*Top*) F.W. Kanehl is the cornet player just over the snare drummer's right shoulder. He had previously been unidentified in this photograph of the early 1900s South Manchester German-American Band. *Courtesy of the Manchester Historical Society.* (*Bottom*) F.W. Kanehl with his family. He looks more mature in this picture, which was taken during the time he was running for selectman as a socialist. *Author's collection.*

First published 2021

Manufactured in the United States

ISBN 9781467148115

Library of Congress Control Number: 2020945790

*To my granddaughters, Makala, Juliet and Hailey, so history can come alive.*

# Contents

# *Introduction*

Stories of Manchester have been part of my life for as long as I can remember. They are stories that drew me into the study of history, and they are stories that I have used in my classrooms to excite students. This book is a collection of some of these stories. But it is more than just a compilation of previous columns that appeared in the *Journal Inquirer*, our local newspaper; it is a collection of strange, interesting facts that need to be persevered for the next generation.

When I was a fifth grader at Green School, which is located on the Green in Manchester, I fell in love with history—but not because of any Hollywood movie or exciting book. No, I fell in love with history because my teacher, Mrs. France, would point out the window and say, "George Washington walked down that road." And he had. I knew this because my grandfather had constructed a monument to Washington's visit at Woodbridge Tavern in November 1789. Mrs. France instantly captured my heart by connecting my history to the history of the nation.

This set of columns was not constructed for historians, but for the new residents of the town who know nothing of Manchester history. They were also constructed for my two youngest granddaughters, both of whom are growing up in Manchester. This work is to be their connection to the history of their family, town and nation.

The columns appear in this book as they were originally printed. I have included a section following each to present any new information, conclusions and exciting reactions the originals generated. Two additional columns

Looking north, or uptown, on Main Street in Manchester. *Postcard from the author's collection.*

tied nicely into articles I produced for the history society's newsletter, so I included them. I also included a small article I wrote for the Manchester Board of Education's website, as it fit the narrative.

What gave me the pedigree to believe I could write a history of the town? I was born and raised in Manchester. My family has been in town for over one hundred years not as a leading family, but as an average go-to-work-daily family. My grandfather built a house for the town's centennial historian, Matthias Spiess. I mowed the lawn of the sesquicentennial historian, William Buckley. After leaving Manchester high school, I earned a degree in history from the University of Connecticut. I then used that knowledge in my journalism career, writing with local papers in both Connecticut and Maine. I also received a master's degree and a sixth year in education while serving as a teacher in Connecticut and Maine. Connecting history through storytelling is a skill set all teachers should use. I have been successful for over thirty years with this approach, whether I have used it in history, science, language arts or math education. I have also served on the boards of the Pitkin Glass Works and the Manchester Historical Society. Despite all of this, most Manchester history people know me as the man at the Old Manchester Museum (OMM). I have been a docent at the OMM for several years, and I hope to see you there one day.

I sincerely hope that this volume will entertain you and make you say, "Oh, I didn't know that!" And if I have forgotten something, please let me know so that I can say the same thing and place it in one of my regular newspaper columns.

# 1

# *Why Manchester*

M ost nonfiction articles on Manchester, Connecticut, will state that the settlement of the area started in the early 1700s as a continuation of the Hartford and East Hartford settlements. An independent Orford Parish was established just after the American Revolutionary War, and it grew into Manchester. Incorporation as a town came in 1823. Most articles will then note that Orford Parish was the location of the Pitkin Glass Works. This factory held a monopoly on glass production in the state for over twenty years in recognition of its production of gun powder for George Washington's troops. Most articles then might mention that the town was also the site of the Cheney Brothers Silk Mills. This venture was one of the largest silk producers in the world. Finally, a listing of famous people, such as Christopher M. Spencer and Geno Auriemma, might follow.

This simple account is all true, but the spirit of the community is missing.

Let's try modifying the textbook approach. Located just ten miles from the state capital, Hartford, Manchester's nickname is the City of Village Charm. It came to dominate the economic development and financial security of the eastern side of the state. It was the home of the largest silk industry in the nation and Bon Ami Soap, and it was the location of smaller thriving mills, agricultural plants and wholesalers that have existed from Manchester's beginnings to now.

Manchester's products filled the average home. A 1900s historian noted with pride that, as he sat in Washington, D.C., products of his native state surrounded him. He also noted that most of the daily objects he used had been constructed in Connecticut mills. I feel that same pride when I look back on the history of my native Manchester. This 1900s historian could have efficiently been addressing just Manchester's economic footprint on the world. Manchester was the site of various mills that produced a wide array of daily essentials, such as paper, silk, wool, needles, musical organs and the filtration systems that are used for water treatment today. This business core had been laid, nurtured and matured over the previous two centuries, providing Manchester with a steady and reliable income, even as the mills closed. The town prospered because of its ability to adjust and overcome. But Manchester was more than an industrial town.

Manchester has no significant natural resource that compelled its development. There are a few small rivers and brooks that were dammed for waterpower, but no large lake or river was present to provide the ease of transportation or energy that was needed for the massive economic development of early America. The town has no harbor that could have called adventurous ships to offload settlers, providing the workforce needed for the future industrial boom. There was not even excellent soil to draw farmers away from other New England agricultural locations, as the town's soil grew more rocks than crops. Manchester itself was a simple plain with rolling hills covered in trees when the Native Americans used the site for hunting and interim camps between their permanent homes. But the fact that there was flat land and smooth hills created Manchester's importance. These natural byways allowed Natives to walk between what is now East Hartford and East Windsor, as well as farther east, toward the great lakes in Ellington and Coventry. Over time, the Natives' progress across these hills and plains created the Great Path.

Manchester became the hub for transportation not just for the Native population but also for the English settlers when they arrived. Mirroring the Natives' trails, the English constructed their roads. Routes 6 and 44 now merge in Manchester and branch off across the state. These "highways" provided easy, direct connections for men and women on foot, in wagons and in cars from the 1600s to today. The interstate highway, which was constructed in the 1950s, also mirrors the trails that were used by the Native Americans in Manchester.

Manchester Green, the original center of the community, was the merging point of the great trails. Here, the tavern was constructed, and the stage line switched horses. Here, the trolley, in its time of commuting dominance, would terminate and then head out to other points on the compass. While it may seem odd, the railroad did not come to the Green, as a more economically based route sent it just south north of the Green, through Unionville, connecting Hartford and Vernon. Today, the state highway still provides easy access to the Green and beyond.

From this kernel of a community and other small settlements along the great path, Manchester grew. Originally, life centered on agriculture and simple milling. The taverns provided a place for residents to hear the latest news and dreams for the new nation. Other residents would come and settle farther and farther from the great trail, but they would stay there permanently. A new town center grew away from the Green as the dominant religion, the Congregationalists, constructed a meetinghouse midway between the various smaller "villes." A second religious group, the Methodists, placed its meetinghouse there as well, and a school developed within this new center. The Green slowly lost its significance, but Manchester continued to be a transportation hub, even with a new center.

Then, in the early 1800s, the center moved once more, toward the man-made lake that had been created from the damming from the Hockanum River for two large mills. One of these mills produced wool, and the other produced paper. Unionville, as this town center was known, was also known as the North End, and it drew not only the large industrial mills, but also the railroad on its way from Hartford to Providence, Rhode Island, and Boston, Massachusetts. This iron horse cemented the North End of Manchester as the economic anchor for the town during the early to mid-1800s.

The Union Woolen Mill employed over four hundred people in its heyday. But like many mills of the 1800s, it was not stable, and bankruptcy affected its management. In time, the financial failures and natural disasters of the area pulled the rug out from under the Union Woolen Mill. Other smaller mills rose to dominance in the area, but like the tide, it ebbed and flowed, and the North End's economic health was off and on. However, small communities continued to prosper around their various mill complexes, from the Hillardville's Wool to the Parkville paper Mills. These small entities waited their turns to become the new centers of the town.

Just after the Civil War, many New England soldiers returned home to pack and leave for the fertile grasslands that they had heard about in the West. This soldier migration drew away between half and two-thirds of New England's population after the war. Manchester, however, did not see such a devastating migration. A new company replaced the Union Company, and its leader, Frank W. Cheney, was a Civil War colonel. His vision for the growth of his family's mill reached across the corporate board table and toward the kitchen tables of the town's residents. Frank became the director of Cheney Brother Silk Mills after the war, and he shepherd it through a growth that peaked in the 1920s, when the mill employed over four thousand townspeople. The silk company rose from one small mill along the banks of Hop Brook to encompass most of South Manchester in physical brick and mortar structures; it also held communal dominance through schools, utilities and economic well-being.

But Manchester was much more than Cheney Brothers. Though they dominated employment, other industrial and commercial entities provided opportunities for the town. These additional financial movers offered economic security to the other three-fourths of Manchester's twenty-five thousand people in the 1920s. The South End also held the paper mills of the Chase Brothers. Parkerville provided the Lydall & Foulds Mills, which produced paper and, later, water filtration units. The Green had the Glastonbury Mill, with its woolen underwear trade. The North End saw the growth of the soap industry under Robertson (Bon Ami) as well as the textile and machine industries, with companies such as Hillard and Adams and Rodgers.

As the century dawned, Manchester was in the best condition to exploit the decade. It had a solid industrial base and an agricultural wing that still provided daily tobacco and landscaping plants for nationwide export. Through two wars and the Great Depression, the town's central silken bond kept it alive. It provided not only employment, but the education workers needed to be adaptable in the years ahead. The Cheney Brothers company died twice: once during the Great Depression, when it cut workers, production and wages, and again after the demand for silk evaporated after World War II's parachute demands. But Manchester continued to grow. Many of the Cheney factory workers found work in the East Harford Pratt and Whitney company and other war industries, which came to replace textiles and paper in Connecticut. Manchester's schools had prepared these workers to adapt.

New generations of residents allowed Manchester to live up to its reputation as the City of Village Charm, as they used the Great Trail to travel to and from work daily. Today, Manchester, ever the transportation hub, contains the primary shopping centers of the region. This started when the commercial center was constructed near the North End train station. Following the rise of the silk industry, this commercial center migrated south along Main Street. Today, the historic buildings that line Main Street appear much as they did one hundred years ago. Photographs and the names that are carved into the buildings' brick and mortar exteriors prove this. The businessmen of the 1800s constructed a boulevard-width road that provided plenty of parking and travel space for the trolley and cars. Today, the width of Main Street remains, and visitors continue to see the same impressive view that was laid out in the late 1800s from Center Congregational Church to the south.

Main Street in Manchester runs from the Glastonbury Line to the train junction in North Manchester. It literally runs up a hill from Glastonbury, reaches a crest at Center Congressional Church and then runs downhill to the old train station. A memoir from the 1920s noted that, when people in the south end of Manchester visited Main Street, they either said that they went "up street or uptown." My aunt always said she went downtown because she had to start at the top of the street; meanwhile south end residents started at the bottom of the road. Residents were therefore either literally going up or down the street, depending on from which end they started.

Seen from the 1900s point of view, the North End's commercial outlets included general stores, a hotel for train passengers, the local newspaper and various other mercantile operations. The South End also had hotels for silk factory visitors, grocery stores, mercantile operations and department stores. Both ends of Main Street had a Catholic church and a Congregational church. It was as if each end was its own separate town, and in the eyes of many, they were. Just as the Green remained an "independent" community, so did the other sections of the town in their own ways. Each section of the town was dominated by a local post office and a general or grocery store. Many times, these two entities were actually operated in the same building.

Northern Main Street had large wooden buildings that ran perpendicular to the train station, which housed the various commercial operations. Residents used these facilities until the mid-1960s, when the town took an urban renewal grant, raised the buildings and reworked the flow of traffic. The South end of Main Street was laid out as a wide boulevard-style road, with multistory brick and wooden buildings lining the eastern side. These buildings remain today, and they have generally gone unchanged since the 1920s, when my grandparents lived in the town. The size and construction of these buildings showed off the wealth that was brought to the town by various industries and maintained by the merchants of the community. My aunt could remember going to one of the department stores in 1914 and charging a winter coat because everyone knew who her father was. This was true of the Cheney daughters and the Rogers children. The merchants knew the citizens.

Religion played its part in the communities. Many of the original denominations can still be seen today, as their structures speak of the devotion other residents mustered over time. The Congregational church located in the center of town is one of the two that are each located in their "centers." The first major town consolidation came with the construction of Center Congregationalist Church. The title of this church is not accurate, as it was constructed long before there was an independent Manchester—it was still part of East Hartford. At the time, the residents of the Manchester area wanted to build a meetinghouse to save on travel to East Hartford's Congregational church. The town fathers of East Hartford were not opposed and sent a group of surveyors to the Manchester area to determine the location of a central church building. The site that was chosen was midway between the East Hartford center and the border of Bolton. The location was on a hill but was still a distance from the population center at the Green. Anger rose among the Manchester people, and eventually, cooler heads moved the church building to where the existing church stands today, at the summit of the Main Street hill. From that time forward, the church has been called the center of town, when in actuality, it is not.

Other denominations followed the Congregationalists, as new immigrant settlers and older residents found fault with the first churches. Today, you can find magnificent stone churches and small wooden churches throughout the town. Many of these structures came about through corporate help, as the mills owners were well aware that to maintain their workforce, they needed to help in communal construction projects. Other churches were established due to the fundraising efforts of devout congregations. Manchester's immigrant heritage can clearly be seen in the names of these congregations, including the Swedish Lutheran Church and the St. John's Polish Catholic Church.

Manchester started as a place of refuge from Hartford. The first settlers in the early 1700s eased over from the East Hartford settlement as they began farming along the Hop Brook. Time brought additional farmers and small grist and lumber mill operations. By the time of the Revolutionary War, several taverns along the Great Path had been established, and the Pitkin family had emerged as the first great industrial giants in the Manchester area. Richard Pitkin founded a powder mill to produce gun powder for the American troops against the British. As payment for this powder, a Manchester legend was born. Pitkin's monopoly on glass and snuff jumpstarted Manchester.

Residents, the Pitkins among them, disgruntled at having to travel to the East Hartford center for voting, meetings and church, petitioned over and over again for a separate parish, and Orford Parish was born. This

These rare glass bottles manufactured at Manchester's Pitkin's Glass Works in the early 1800s demonstrate the skill of the local artisans. *Courtesy of the Manchester Historical Society.*

consolidation, almost a township inside a township, continued to request more independence, and in 1823, it earned that right and became Manchester.

A textbook history of the town would end here, with little acknowledgement of the men and women who actually made Manchester what it is today. But this book is not a textbook; it is an attempt to bring to life those people and happenings which make the town's history a story instead of a list of facts and dates.

# 2

# Beginnings

*Additional information on "Manchester's" (column's topic) can be found at the Old Manchester Historical Museum, located at 126 Cedar Street. Come to visit. It is open on the first Saturday of each month (May through December) from 10:00 a.m. to 2:00 p.m. I'll see you there.*

## THE STORY OF THE BUCKLAND DINOSAUR

Long before there were human footprints in the freshly fallen snow of winter in Manchester, there were footprints of animals. Animals that you know today—squirrels, foxes and rabbits—filled the woods around the house you might live in today. But centuries before now, dinosaurs roamed in the woods of this area. Yes, Manchester had dinosaurs. In fact, there was a dinosaur that lived in Manchester that was unique to the area.

Manchester occupies ground that was once a large lake and marshy area. The marsh's red mud became the large red stone cliffs that you can see today as you drive toward the mall and the highway to Hartford. Dinosaurs lived here when the rock was mud, and their bones were preserved as fossils when the mud became sedimentary rock. As time has passed, the pressure pushing down on the mud created sedimentary rocks. Anything that may have died in the mud became encased in the new stone and was transformed into a fossil. The Connecticut Valley region is famous for its sedimentary rocks, which often have footprints and bones trapped inside. Manchester is in the valley and has its rocky remembrance of the time before time.

Red Stone fossil located in a doorstep of a one-hundred-year-old home. *Author's photograph.*

The Smithsonian Museum in Washington, D.C., notes that the discovery of East Coast dinosaurs is rare because people have been building on this part of the country for hundreds of years. This fact made the discovery of an almost complete skeleton here in Manchester even more impressive. These bones were excavated in the 1880s and 1890s. The men who worked at the Wolcott Quarry in the Buckland area of Manchester made the find. The discoveries were analyzed and categorized by the leading dinosaur hunter (archaeologist) of the time, Yale University professor Othniel Charles Marsh. Marsh named the three different animals *Anchisaurus colorus*, *Anchisaurus solus* and *Anchisaurus major*. He noted that these early Jurassic-era dinosaurs ranged in length from about six feet to thirteen feet, and he said that they were capable of rising on their hind feet to reach the tree leaves they ate.

Now, it gets crazy, as history is never finished and continuously changing. The Manchester bones were moved to the Peabody Museum at Yale University, where they were listed as herbivores (plant-eating) dinosaurs. Scientists and historians are never satisfied, however, and over the years, people have reviewed these rare specimens. Over time, professors agreed that all the specimens were actually from the same family of dinosaurs, which they now call *Anchisaurus polyzelu*. Scientists have tied the Manchester dinosaurs to others found throughout the Connecticut River Valley, each with little differences. Still, they all have enough similarities to make them part of the same family.

But history is still not settled. These Manchester dinosaurs may have had an even more critical position in the development of history than Professor Marsh had thought. The latest belief is that these Manchester residents used their front legs as hands to grab and hold things. They even had a digit that appears to be similar to a thumb. Not only could they grab with their front paws, their jaws were designed with some pointed teeth, and they had forward-facing eyes, both of which hint at an ability to hunt and eat meat. They could have been the first dinosaur that bridged the gap between plant- and meat-eaters. The Manchester dinosaur now carries an omnivore label.

The fossils now rest at the Yale Peabody Museum in New Haven, alongside a majority of Professor Marsh's other significant discoveries. The nearly complete skeleton of the Manchester dinosaur is still viewable.

But not all of Manchester's fossils are located in a museum. There is a rumor in history that says some of the fossils were used to construct a bridge in town. Whether the bridge was built over the Hop Brook or the Bigelow Brook is a matter of debate, but neither bridge stands today. What happened to the fossils?

## *Afterword*

After this column appeared, I received a few phone calls concerning the sandstone bridge removals for the highway. One caller had been present when the bridge came down but did not see any fossils. Another caller claimed that there had been various professor-like officials at the bridge removal, and they said that some rocks had been examined and removed. Either way, I feel the mystery remains. However, I have to admit that, in the fifty years since the removal of the sandstone bridges in Manchester, no public collections have announced the display of Manchester fossils.

# Manchester's Footprint Covers a Wide Swath of Territory, Sparks Pride

Growing up in Manchester, I developed a healthy pride in the town and my schools. Remarkable Manchester personalities, innovations and incidents filtered through the years, nourishing this pride as I discovered Manchester's footprint wherever I lived in other states and towns. This column is my attempt to pass that pride along to my grandchildren and the new residents of Manchester.

One of these strings of pride filled me one summer evening as I stood in the rose garden at Deering Oaks Park in Portland, Maine. The large park is located north of Portland's Old Port. It has served the city well over the years, providing respite and a gathering place for the residents. Its charm was even captured in the poem "My Lost Youth," which was written in the 1800s by Portland's own Henry Wadsworth Longfellow. So, it was with great pride that I found among the identified species of roses, the First Lady rose. The Burr Nursery developed this rose right here in Manchester.

Clifford Burr and his son Charles created the nursery just north of the Apel Opera House on Oakland Street. For years, the company was famous for its bush and ornamental trees. Burr filled orders from around the world. The elder Burr's interest in horticulture was focused on native and landscaping plants. The younger Burr was drawn to the cultivation of flowers and, in particular, roses. The rose I discovered in Portland's garden a few years ago was developed in honor of two presidents' wives. This just goes to show that Manchester has a rich history that has affected more people than its residents.

Another moment when my hometown pride overcame me occurred while I was teaching in Norway, Maine. When reviewing the textbook that I used for the student's understanding of American history, I discovered an image that I had seen too many times to count. Located in the Civil War chapter was a reproduction of a painted portrait of Dorothea Dix. For those not familiar with American Civil War history, Dix was the head of the Union army's nursing corps. After the war, she became an advocate for the mentally insane. She was a native of Maine. Dixville, Maine, was named for her family. So, it was natural for this painting to be used in a textbook in that state.

What the book selecting committee did not know, however, was that the artist of the painting was Manchester's, Seth Cheney. A similar reproduction of the portrait is located in William Buckley's *History of Manchester: A New*

F.W. Kanehl is the cornet player just over the snare drummer's right shoulder. He had previously been unidentified in this photograph of the early 1900s South Manchester German-American Band. *Courtesy of the Manchester Historical Society.*

*England Pattern.* I had seen it over and over throughout the years each time I reviewed Manchester history. I just could not believe that I would see that same picture in isolated Norway, Maine.

My students soon had a second Manchester Civil War connection in their history class: the story of Manchester's native Christopher Spencer and his repeating rifle. The rifle used so effectively at the Battle of Gettysburg that General Custer's outnumbered Michigan Brigade outshot J.E.B. Stuart's army.

A final Manchester footprint that stands out in my mind is the glass bottle display at Old Sturbridge Village. The students I took to that living museum had to hear how I grew up just down the road from the ruins of the factory. Today, you can still walk past the same structure I did—a vacant stone-walled hint of the prosperity of early Manchester.

As they say—it is a small world, and we are all connected.

# UNCOVER SOMETHING NEW, AND WATCH HISTORY CHANGE BEFORE YOUR VERY EYES

I tell my grandchildren that history is an ever-changing discipline. They look on in disbelief, as most people do. To them, history is the memorization of dates and times; you know, that boring class material they suffered through in school. How can history be changing, they ask, when it has already happened? But history is much more than dates and times. It is the story of people. As a volunteer at the Old Manchester Museum, I see that story every time I look at the displays. Not only is it the story of people, but it is also a story of rediscovered sources.

A few years ago, I wrote the book *Hannah's Ghost*. The book's premise is that the main character finds the solution to an actual historical mystery in the attic of her grandfather's house. The mystery was about who painted the only representation of Tapping Reeve, the founder of the first law school in America. This real mystery haunted the Litchfield, Connecticut Historical Society for years. Then, shortly after the publication of my fiction book, a discovery in an attic in a Pennsylvania house brought out the truth. Believe it or not, my guess as a writer was correct; the person I attributed the work of art to was the actual painter, according to the newfound source. Even in Manchester, we can suddenly rewrite history.

One night, when I was in high school, my father received a phone call from people he didn't know. They identified themselves as the owners of the old Mathias Spiess house. It seemed that they had been stripping the wallpaper from their living room and discovered some writing they felt my father might have been interested in seeing. My father had once said that his father, my grandfather, had been friends with the town historian Spiess, but he could not prove it. He also said that my grandfather had constructed the houses in the area around where Mathias Spiess lived. When we arrived at the house, the couple showed us the living room. There, written on the wall in bold handwriting, was "Wall papered by August and F. William Kanehl, 1933, the night that Hitler became chancellor of Germany." It was often the case for painters of that time to make a note on the wall before covering it with wallpaper. That one sentence confirmed what my father had only believed. History had changed.

My father was one who said he loved history, but when it came to his own family, he appeared to have other thoughts. He said he was a mistake, as his parents were in their fifties when he was born. Most of his uncles were already dead, having died when they were young men. This fact left him without a strong knowledge of his family history. When I was young, he told me that his father and his uncle August were the only two Kanehls to come to Connecticut from Germany. Imagine my disbelief when I found not just my grandfather's grave in East Cemetery, but the graves of three other Kanehls—all brothers of my grandfather. These men all died when my father was under the age of six. No wonder their history became forgotten with their burials.

I am still trying to patch together a new family tree for my granddaughters to plant. Imagine what family "history" you can rediscover with a little research yourself. Maybe you can find a clue that will rewrite history.

## 3
## *What's Old Is News Again*

### THE CURRENT CRISIS MAKES US WONDER ABOUT THE FLU PANDEMIC OF 1918 AND 1919

"No school today?" my granddaughter asked as she talked to me on the phone. OK, we were video chatting, as she wanted to see my wife and me, but her mother had said she could not see us in person—cautions for the coronavirus. My wife noted that this situation was the strangest thing to have occurred in her life. My superintendent of schools said that, no matter who she asked for advice, no one was old enough to have been around the last time Connecticut faced an impending epidemic. That happened over one hundred years ago, and Manchester's reaction was similar to the rest of the nation and was almost the same as we see today.

Near the end of the First World War, influenza struck the soldiers in Europe. The illness was called the "Spanish flu" because Spain was not fighting in the war and the uncensored Spanish press was the first to carry stories of the flu. With the returning soldiers, influenza came to America. There were two strains of the 1918 flu: one killed with a high fever and one killed with pneumonia. Victims of the high fever–oriented strain died quickly, while the other had victims lingering for months. Manchester saw its fever victims dying within three days, according to a history society account of C. Elmore Walkins. It was Walkins who helped create Manchester Hospital in 1920, a response to the town's needs and realizations brought on by influenza.

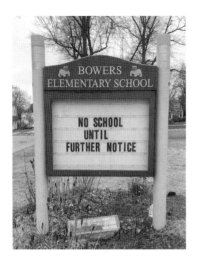

Residents were greeted by this "school closing" sign in Manchester in March 2020. *Author's photograph.*

In this same write-up, Dr. George Lundberg of Manchester, who was then interning in Philadelphia, noted that "the disease rapidly spread from one part of the country to another." The nation "suddenly realized that they were in the midst of a severe epidemic of influenza, such as occurred in 1890. Thousands of new cases were being reported every 24 hours. Bodies began piling up at the cemeteries because of the sheer inability to bury them as fast as they came."

In Connecticut, cities set up emergency hospitals to handle the people infected. At least a quarter of the population was estimated to be affected, with the young and healthy men and women hit the hardest. Unlike the present epidemic, which attaches itself to older residents, in 1918 and 1919, it was the middle-aged and young adults who suffered the most. In Manchester, the sick remained at home because there were no other services available besides family care and doctor visits. Walkins recalled that the town had about eight doctors at the time—mostly older men—and very few nurses. "The main problem was to find anyone to do anything for the sick—not a doctor, not a trained nurse, but any able-body person." Walkins opened a Red Cross office and "did a great deal of telephoning for afflicted families." This service ran day and night in search of healthcare workers. Walkins also noted that masked residents met visitors to their houses throughout the town.

"When we seemed to be at the lowest ebb one morning," Walkins wrote, "Frank Anderson, vice president of the chapter in charge of civilian relief and Frank Cheney came into my office with a breathless announcement." Cheney Brothers made the first floor of Cheney Hall available as a temporary hospital, with one doctor and nurse to supervise. This emergency hospital had beds for fifty people. "Once our emergency hospital opened, there was a constant succession of cars bringing in the sick, and we are sorry to report a few ambulances and hearses taking them away." Walkins concludes that the goal of the makeshift hospital "was to save the lives of many people."

Less than a year later, the town appointed a committee to honor the servicemen and women of Manchester who had fought in World War I. This

Today's Manchester Memorial Hospital front only hints at the original structure. *Author's photograph.*

show of honor, which came so shortly after the influenza epidemic, took the shape of the Manchester Memorial Hospital. A ceremony on November 22, 1919, set the cornerstone for the current building.

## THE HOSPITAL CAME ABOUT AS WAR MEMORIAL AND RESPONSE TO 1918 FLU PANDEMIC

Coming out of a dance show, one of my granddaughters noticed the large brass plaque of names on the wall just outside the auditorium at the Manchester High School. On the wall are three Kanehls. She wanted to know who they were and why her name was on the wall. "That is the honor roll for the Second World War," I explained. "These are the names of men who served during the war." She nodded and asked if all the schools had such walls. I shook my head and took her to a different building with a wall of names, but the memorial is the whole building, not just the plaque of names.

A hundred years ago, Manchester was looking for a way to honor the men and women from the town who served the nation during the First World War, especially the forty-three who did not return. A committee formed that developed the concept of a living memorial—the hospital. The entire hospital and its operations are a World War I memorial.

Originally, the idea of constructing a hospital in town grew out of the great influenza epidemic of 1918 and 1919. This flu caused one in every four American residents to get sick and caused the deaths of millions worldwide. My aunt remembered that the Cheney Brothers opened the Cheney Hall to serve as a hospital in the crises. This arrangement allowed the sick to be treated in isolation, preventing the remainder of their family members from getting infected. Manchester's use of Cheney Hall to isolate the infected may have caused the flu to be eradicated quickly in the town. According to the town historians, the flu, which erupted around the country for nearly a year, was only vicious during the fall of 1918 and mostly disappeared with the coming winter.

The fact that there was no central place for the treatment of the sick and injured helped focus the idea of honoring the returning war veterans with a hospital. The committee suggested that a fifty-bed hospital be constructed for the residents of Manchester for $150,000. Within a month, that amount of money was raised; in fact, local businesses and community residents pledged over $200,000. On November 22, 1919, the builders set the cornerstone, and the actual hospital opened for patients on Armistice Day, November 11, 1920. For years, the hospital was called Manchester Memorial Hospital, reinforcing the idea that it was constructed as a living memorial. Now, it is a member of the Eastern Connecticut Health Network, but the history remains.

Today, inside the hospital's main hallway, there are two brass plaques listing the names of the honored residents of Manchester who responded to their nation's call to war. Originally, they stood in the doorway of the original main lobby of the hospital, but they have since moved with various construction projects.

Members of the Manchester community provided funding for the fifty-bed memorial hospital; this funding ranged from sponsoring the purchase furniture to offering to finance whole rooms. Initially, name plaques were placed outside the doors of the various places that were sponsored by members of the community; they were placed as a way to remember the efforts of these residents. Among the donators were the Cheney family, which anonymously donated funding for the kitchens and other facilities. Not only did male members of the Cheney family fight for the nation, but three of the Cheney daughters (Dorothy, Marjorie and Emily) also volunteered as nurses near the front lines. Other female Manchester residents, such as Bessie Anderson, also served on the front lines as nurses.

## *Afterword*

It is hard to imagine that the past two articles I wrote about the influenza outbreak and the one I wrote for the one hundredth birthday of the Manchester Hospital foreshadowed the coronavirus outbreak of 2020. The following is a short piece I wrote for our local board of education website. It focuses on my reaction to the state's first two weeks of shutdown and the start of distance learning that we developed for our students.

# CHANGE IN WORKLOAD—WHAT CHANGE?

When the governor closed down the schools in the state for two weeks, it was to prevent the spread of the virus. This closure was seen as a preemptive step in preventing students from contaminating each other, teachers and their families. As a historian who had studied the 1918 and 1919 flu, I was aware that schools in Manchester did not shut down during that pandemic until Superintendent Fred Verplanck felt that too many teachers were absent. Today is a different time. One hundred years ago, there had to be person-to-person contact in daily life, which helped spread influenza. Today, because of the internet and the advancement of other technologies, we can live an independent life.

I am a teacher—not in Manchester but in Willimantic. How strange is it that Verplanck had come from Willimantic to Manchester, while I was doing the opposite. Either way, the two weeks, as far as I saw it, would be made up in June, so to me, these two weeks were the beginning of my summer break.

Like all good husbands who are teachers, I looked to my wife for a list of jobs around the house that had to be done when I had the free time—the dreaded summer honey-do list. The first thing on the agenda this year was the removal of our old wall-to-wall carpet. This carpet removal was how we spent the first four days of the shutdown, on our hands and knees, pulling carpet, nailing sticks and staples—boy, were there staples. To our surprise, beautiful wooden floors were under the padding. All it needed was a little sanding and finishing. Guess what the second week of the shutdown focused on?

Meanwhile, I continued to write my history column for the newspaper. I even helped launch the distance learning for my school. This distance learning came to fill my days with meetings and then preparing and correcting schoolwork for my students. The components of distance learning were nothing that we had not already done, from video chats to online assignments, et cetera. This time, however, we focused on these assignments for the school's entire population, not just a few students.

After two weeks, my daily routine became schoolwork again. The only difference was that, instead of leaving Manchester at 6:30 a.m. each morning, I got to exercise then go to my office in my house to conduct a class. In general, other than the fact that we did not visit anyone or attend meetings (yes, I was a member of the board of directors who held the first virtual meeting), life in my household did not change much because of the virus precautions.

Only two things have stood out as truly different. One is my wife's constant shaking of her head and saying, "This is the strangest thing I have ever lived through." The other is the fact that I had time to prepare another book manuscript for the publishers well ahead of the time expected.

After this article appeared on the town web page, the governor closed the schools for another month, and then until the end of the school year. My time was spent working with students through virtual meetings. The students who did not sign into these chat times were helped through email and directions given through my daily classroom assignments.

Again, I am amazed at how well the state functioned in reducing the number of citizens who got sick in the stay-at-home period. This decrease was due to the fact that we could function and be somewhat productive without the face-to-face contact. Technology is the big winner for us today when compared to the millions who were infected in 1918 and 1919.

# 4

# *Town Features*

## THE POST OFFICES HAVE RICH AND "SCATTERED" HISTORY

I took my granddaughter to the Buckland Post Office the other day, and she asked why it was so small compared to the one on Sheldon Road. I smiled and recalled growing up, when we had the large post office at the center of town, one in Buckland and the other small one located midway down Broad Street.

Once, when I was a young father, my oldest son saw a rabbit the night before Easter behind the old Buckland Post Office (now a bank). He instantly knew someone was going to be visiting him soon. I played up that memory for years whenever he began to disbelieve.

Manchester has had many buildings designated as post offices throughout its history. Initially, most of the post offices took up a corner inside a general store or tavern. One such building at the Green is now a restaurant. Even the original Highland Park Market hosted a post office. Some were designated their own buildings in various locations by the postmasters, like Olin Gerich Sr., a friend of my father. He ran the Buckland Area Post Office from inside his service station. The station is still there and is still owned by the Gerich family.

Other locations of Manchester post offices included the family house on the corner of Hillstown Road and Hills Street. The postmaster of

Post office desk from the Manchester Green Post Office, part of the society's exhibit. *Courtesy of the Manchester Historical Society.*

West Manchester rented out a small room in the house between the 1880s and early 1900s. North Manchester, or Manchester Station, had its own post office site because of the train station that connected the world to Manchester. It was across the street from the station in one of the buildings that was removed during the town's redevelopment of the 1960s.

The opening of these post office locations coincided with the opening of small villages and stagecoach stops, which sprang up in the general area that is known today as Manchester. They served the population, which could not travel far. Transportation developments and consolidation brought the small post office heyday to a close.

As the town grew, the smaller post office centralized its operation. The main post office opened in the round-ish building that dominated one corner of the Main and East Center Street intersection. This building was constructed during the Great Depression era and is now the Weiss office building, named for Robert Weiss, the longtime town manager. This building served the town's postal needs for decades, including the two outside drop-off mailboxes. I remember them well. During tax season, my father often had me ride with him so that he could pull into one of the "unofficial" parking spaces near the boxes. I would jump out of the car, race down the street and mail whatever tax returns or extensions were due. There were even times when I had to sit in the car while he went into the post office to get a mailing stamped. Oh, the joy of being "grown-up" enough to guard the vehicle in the no-parking space.

Modernization led to the construction of the facility on Sheldon Road. This site provided parking for patrons and postal vehicles. Its design emulates the other post offices that were constructed in the surrounding towns during the 1980s. It was opened in 1991.

Fortunately, the central post office has not gotten rid of the smaller, more convenient drop-off satellite office in Buckland. There are times during the year when this smaller facility is a welcome destination, even if it is a bit of a longer ride.

## When Trolleys Were the Way to Go

My granddaughters love watching the school bus drop students off near my house. They are among the lucky few who walk to school, and they will walk to school for most of their public-school career.

Busses dominate our cross-town travel now, but one hundred years ago, it was the trolley that transported most people across town or even town to town. Manchester had its share of trolley lines, and the tracks themselves were still visible in my youth on Main Street. But today, like the railroad, trolley cars are a rare sight. The girls think of trolleys as most children do today, as a character on Mr. Rogers.

I spent this past summer at the Connecticut Trolley Museum in East Windsor learning to drive the vehicles. I discovered that electrical engineering truly hasn't changed over the one hundred years of trolley development. The electrical trolleys of 1890 operated on the same principles as the trolleys of today. It is the outward appearance that has changed, as well as the use.

At one time, it was a daily occurrence for the residents of Manchester to travel around town, to Hartford or Rockville, on the trolley. They were the buses of the day. Horace Wickham and Maro Chapman started Manchester's trolley system. Tracks ran the length of Main Street (north to south) and Center Street, from the Green Area to East Hartford, and connections merged in several locations for trips outside of Manchester. Eventually,

Main Street, Looking South, South Manchester, Conn.

The trolley makes its way down Main Street from the town center. *Postcard from the author's collection.*

Manchester's tracks became part of the Hartford-to-Rockville Line, a branch of which is maintained by the Trolley Museum in East Windsor to provide a little reenactment for visitors and drivers. The Connecticut Company took over the local tracks in the 1930s and 1940s. This company converted the trolleys lines into bus routes, still servicing the town.

Two things struck me while at the museum this summer. The first was that many trolley companies developed amusement parks that could only be accessed by riding the trolley. In East Windsor, an example of this was Piney Ridge Park. This amusement center became famed for its bouncing dance floor and baseball park. Many early Yankee greats used this field as an alternative diamond when the New York team was not playing. Manchester had its own Laurel Park. Swan boats, long walks, a merry-go-round and zoo animals met the trolley riders. Riding in the open trolley cars in the summer months, speeding along at twenty-five miles per hour, cut the summer heat almost as much as the beer that awaited the riders at the park. Laurel Park sat on the Manchester border with East Hartford, which is across the street from Wickham Park today.

The second fascinating fact I discovered was that trolleys were once used as high school busses. Many students traveled to and from their local high schools aboard the vehicles. If this is true, then Manchester students first used the trolley to get themselves to the North End, where they took a special train to Hartford to attend Hartford Public. Later, they would have traveled on the Main Street Line to the large brick building that was constructed in 1910 across from Bennet Academy. The story at the Trolley Museum is that, on snow days, students had to wake up, dress appropriately and then trough through the snow to the trolley stop. If the car came with a flag on the back, there was no school, and the students troughed home. Maybe that was the start of my father's saying: "I walked to school uphill both ways through the snow."

One question remains at the museum and also in my mind. It is for any who traveled to school on the trolley to answer: What color was the flag? Railroad and trolley rules state specific messages for a red, blue and green flags. Any ideas?

## *Afterword*

My father also remembered that at the end of World War II, some celebrators ran gasoline down the middle of the Main Street tracks and set it on fire. At the time, the trolleys had long stopped traveling the route.

Another reader informed me that the flags on trolley cars were similar to those used on trains. The colors each had their own meanings, including the famed blue flag, which meant that the vehicle could not be moved unless a repairman removed the flag. This reader still could not answer the question about what signal or flag denoted that there was no school.

Yet another reader shared that he had a piece of the trolley tracks from Main Street. He explained that when the town dug up the tracks to resurface Main Street, he ventured out of his office and took a piece home. It will sit in his home until he decides what he will finally do with it.

# At 100 Years: Army and Navy Club on Main Street May be Nation's Oldest Veteran's Organization

My granddaughter noticed the signs on the Army and Navy Club announcing a one-hundred-year celebration. She was wondering if the celebration was for the club or the building. It was for both. The official birthday occurred

The Army Navy Club has been located in this building on Main Street for one hundred years. *Author's photograph.*

in May 1919. It is a birth date that places a building and an organization in a position that may surpass a national organization that was founded by the son of a president.

On Main Street, next to (depending on how old you are) the old high school, Bennet's Main Building or the Bennet Apartments, stands a small building, the Army and Navy Club. It's an organization that grew out of the wishes of Manchester residents to never forget the soldiers and sailors who served not just during the First World War but in all wars. Longtime member Nate Agostinelli noted that the Manchester Army and Navy Club was a unique organization. He could only recall one other club in the whole nation like it. It was the brainchild of the Manchester residents; it was to honor the men who had ventured to France for their country, and it was to provide a center for their friendships to continue.

The original idea for the club was immediately agreed on and paid for by the Manchester Chapter of the Red Cross. The Cheney Brothers provided the land, and local builders and suppliers provided the labor and materials. Within weeks after receiving the blueprints, the volunteers completed the structure you see on Main Street. William Buckley described the project in his book on the history of Manchester: "For about two weeks, the corner of Main and Forest [Streets] was as busy as a hive of bees. The usual schedule of working hours was scrapped. Trucks unloaded piles of lumber. The whines of saws splintered the air, and hammers pounded out their muted anvil chorus. In about two weeks, the building was completed." The building you see on Main Street today is that same structure, although it has sustained a little refurbishing over the years. Imagine a public works project today taking just weeks to go from design to completion.

On May 17, 2019, the building and the club officially turned one hundred years old, marking the date the organization received the clubhouse. This is also the birthday of the American Legion, which claims its inception took place at an officer's meeting in March 1919 among men who were still in France. The national organization was officially chartered in September of that same year. Manchester's local post was chartered in 1924. It is possible to say that the Manchester's Army and Navy Club may be older than the national American Legion organization.

Famous World War I veterans Teddy Roosevelt Jr. and General Wild Bill Donovan founded the American Legion. It was established to provide a place that honored veterans and provided them with a social gathering place. This organization stretched across the nation to honor the men and, later, women who had served during various time frames in the American Armed Forces.

Growing up in town as the son of a veteran, I knew of three organizations that pulled its members from the armed forces: the American Legion, the Veterans of Foreign Wars (VFW) and Manchester's own Army and Navy Club. The VFW was founded to honor those men and, later, women, who left the confines of this country to serve overseas during war. This rule of membership made my father, who stood on Korean soil in wartime, eligible for VFW membership. However, his cousin, who came under hostile fire while chasing Poncho Villa along the Mexican border, could only be a member of the American Legion.

Manchester's Army and Navy Club was different, however. From its beginnings, it welcomed all people who had put on an American service uniform. It was open to anyone who had, as my marine nephew once said, "signed their name and risked their lives in spirit or [in actuality]." According to Agostinelli, it was a veterans' organization that, from day one, was open to any veteran, male or female, if they wished to join. He believes that the first female veteran to join was a nurse from World War II. Though time has brought national changes to both the VFW and Legion, the Manchester Army and Navy Club still rings true as a thank-you to all the servicemen and women of the town.

# A RECENTLY SOLD BUILDING BEGAN AS A HUB OF ENTERTAINMENT

"You mean the Opera House." This statement of fact came from an older resident as I explained to my granddaughter that the Connecticut Co-operative Farmers Feed Association Inc. (COOP) building had been sold. According to the developers, the large brick building located on Apel and Oakland Streets, along with the more modern grain elevator facility, would be transformed from a retail space to apartments and manufacturing space. It started its life as an opera house. Yes, an opera house right here in Manchester.

Constructed in 1887, the opera house was the brainchild of Bernard Apel. This Manchester resident had made his money as a local undertaker and furniture salesman. He envisioned his new building not only serving his furniture business on the first floor, but also hosting local entertainers on the upper floors. With this purpose in mind, Apel incorporated a stage, seating for one thousand and a large dance hall in the design of his building. According to newspaper articles of the time, the construction of the building "used some of the longest lumber ever brought to town." An earlier report from 1878 outlined the impending structure and expressed that Apel's would be the first brick building constructed in the town. That article must have been referring to just the North End of Manchester because Cheney Hall, a brick building, was built in 1867.

Local amateur acting companies based in churches and social clubs began using the upper floor of the building almost instantly after completion. The large brick building quickly became known as Apel's Opera House, a name it continues to own to this day. The label of opera house, according to other historical articles, was used throughout the country for small theaters. Whether it was a means of drawing in professional stock troops to rural communities or was a method of drawing spectators is not explained. Apel's building succeeded on both accounts.

Aside from local entrainers, the hall was rented out over the years to professional touring companies, providing professional shows and concerts to residents. The North End residents of Manchester felt that the site rivaled the South End's Cheney Hall. While Cheney Hall hosted lectures and community events, Apel's staged boxing matches, numerous lighthearted comedies and even New York burlesque shows. One production of the ever-popular *Uncle Tom's Cabin* included two Topsies to "increase the comedy element," according to town historian William Buckley.

The Apel's Opera House of North Manchester, which is currently undergoing a remodeling. *Author's photograph.*

Apel's dance hall was just as famous as its stage. According to the newspaper articles of the time, the Opera House provided the floor for the first masquerade ball in town. The 1891 event, thrown by the Manchester 91 Club, drew in over one hundred costumed residents while packing the hall with spectators. This building was also the location of the town's first movie presentation. The show was presented to help a local club to raise money. Before the consolidation of town schools, the opera house also hosted the graduations from the Eighth District schools.

The opera house was so successful that even after a devastating fire in 1899, Apel had the building rebuilt and then, in 1892, he remodeled it again to include two large chambers for dance and new upholstery for the seats.

Apel, himself died in 1908, and his Opera House faded away. The brick building became a space for various retail stores and warehousing. In 1942, the Central Connecticut Cooperative Farmers Association purchased the site. A new generation came to remember the building for its summer grain aroma and not the roar of laughter.

# The History Behind the Cheney Library Is Much More than Meets the Eye

The Cheney name dominates Manchester history, and my granddaughters have noticed that it still is prevalent today. Even though the last mill closed in the 1970s, the Cheneys' silken hands still reach out across time and mold the young minds of the town.

One of my family's favorite haunts is the Mary Cheney Library. Aside from the economic life their mills brought to the town, the Cheneys were credited with creating a society—what we call social engineering today—that provided a community environment around the mill complex that included not only the nuclear family (millworkers) but also family members (townspeople). An example of this extended community idea is reflected in the history of the Mary Cheney Library.

The original books gathered for the institution were designed to increase production at the mills. The brothers discovered as early as 1843 that if one worker was allowed to read to the others in a group of spinners, more silk was produced than if no one read during a day's work. This same idea was also used in the cigar-rolling factories of Cuba from the mid-1800s to modern times. A reader would be brought into the cigar room, where they sat, reading the local newspaper, magazines or books as the remaining cigar rollers worked.

At Cheney Brothers, the spinners were divided into groups of five. Four ladies would work on the silk while the fifth companion would read from a book provided by the factory. This group of workers would rotate the reader as the days progressed, offering a chance for every spinner to be the reader. In Manchester, this process was used in the early 1800s until the machines became too loud. By the 1850s, the books gathered by the mills were placed in a "library" in Cheney Hall for mill employees to borrow. After a few years, these books, then a well-sized collection, were transferred to a larger building that was purchased by the company on Main Street next to the District Nine School complex. At this time, in the 1880s, the collection was offered to the residents of South Manchester to borrow.

When the school burned down in 1913, the library building also burned. The books, however, were saved by the gathered millworkers who fought the blaze. For a time, the books were returned to Cheney Hall until another house on Main Street could be purchased. There, the ever-expanding collection was housed until it was moved to the current Mary Cheney Library at 586 Main Street.

The Mary Cheney Library dominates Center Memorial Park on Main Street. *Author's photograph.*

The current brick building is located at the center of town and sits on land that was donated by the Cheney family to the city. The 1937 structure was designed and constructed as a WPA project during the Great Depression. Besides donating the property, the Cheney family provided much of the local financial share through money they had set aside for a similar project in the 1920s. Their hands were also on the blueprints, as it was a descendant of the family, Frank C. Farley, who was the project's architect. It is neat to note that Farley's grandmother was the Cheney who donated the land for Center Park in 1905.

Today, all the residents of the town are welcome to become members of the library and borrow the books, extending Cheney's mill family well beyond its millworkers.

Besides books, the library is also the overseer of the Cheney endowment for art and culture. In conjunction with the Cheney Homestead, the library has been given funds to promote arts and culture, as well as encourage young ladies to pursue their dreams.

Aside from the library, the Cheney family's reach can also be seen in various churches, community infrastructure, and financial welfare. But Manchester is much more than just Cheney Silk. Other threads have tied the community together over the years: Pitkin Glassworks, Case Paper, Bon Ami Soap, Rogers Paper, Lydall Paper, Glastonbury, Oakwood and Union Mill, to name a few that have dominated the town.

## *Afterword*

Manchester has more than one library. The North End hosts the Whiton Memorial Library. This institution's original book collection grew from a private association. From the 1860s onward, a membership library had been collecting reading material. Around the turn of the century, the association was struggling, and the King's Daughters of the North Congregational Church took over the collection. At first, it was kept in a small house on North Main Street before it was moved to the Eighth District school building.

Doctor Francis Whiton was determined to have a public library in the town. As part of his 1922 will, he bequeathed money for an independent library structure to be built in the North End. This wealth was large enough to build a two-story brick building with a theater and lecture hall in the basement. It was completed and dedicated in 1932. There was also enough inheritance for the library to purchase volumes of reading material and invest a sizable annuity for future expansion.

What is interesting is that Whiton so wanted the facility located in this part of town that his will specified that none of the inheritance could ever be used by the town for any purchase of library-oriented material or construction housed outside of the North End. Over the years, the North End has prospered with over $1 million from this generous physician.

Whiton Library, located on North Main Street, was the dream of Dr. Whiton. *Author's photograph.*

# "A Hundred Years Ago" Seems More Recent Than It Used to Be

One hundred years ago this year (2018, at the time this article was published), the Yankees came marching home from World War I. Well, not really—they came home in almost the same way that we come back today, by automobiles, buses, trains and planes. It's true that the idea of one hundred years used to mean changes in lifestyles and culture, but one hundred years ago today, the First World War came to an end, and it was broadcasted around the world by telephone, telegraph and radio. The men and women who marched off to war from Manchester in 1916 saw just about the same buildings we do as they walked their way up Main Street from the armory by the newly constructed Bennet Academy. Along their route were many of the buildings that still greet us (House & Hales, Walkins and Johnson Block).

The massive Cheney factory complex was already standing, waiting with open arms for the soldiers to come home. Manchester was already well on its way to becoming the height of the Cheney Mills. It was excepting of the

Manchester's center has changed very little from this 1914 aerial view. *Author's image collection.*

diversity interwoven within the borders of the town. The same welcome that met my immigrant grandparents met me as a child, and it is the same welcome my granddaughters know today. The Manchester of a hundred years ago was not that different from the Manchester of today.

When I was a young boy in elementary school and they talked about one hundred years ago, they talked about the Civil War soldiers coming home by foot, wagon and horseback. The Civil War was a century before my elementary school days, and the break from my world to that one was a real cultural break. During the time of the Civil War, Main Street was dirt-covered. The local buildings were small and far between. The town's houses were generally attached to a barnyard that had a small shelter for the family cow and horse. All of this was hard for me to imagine in the 1960s. For my father, the time of settling and exploring the Louisiana Purchase took place one hundred years before his school days, and for my grandparents, the start of the United States itself occurred one hundred years before their school days.

My granddaughters now don't see that clear break of one hundred years; like today, jazz and records were heard when the doughboys came home. Motion pictures were in vogue. Manchester had two movie theaters then. Civil War soldiers could hardly understand the new invention of the photograph, let alone imagine moving pictures. Airplanes and automobiles were easing horses and buggies off the road. One hundred years ago, my grandfather invested in a Mack chain-driven truck for his building business. This investment came as he expanded with the coming of the new decade after the First World War.

To the soldiers of the Civil War, Christmas was something of a new practice. It was then a Victorian concept that was creeping its way into the American way of life with Prince Albert's Germanic Christmas tree. One hundred years before my youthful days, Charles Dickens's stories were filtering through the simplistic Puritan celebrations that were still present in many New England towns. But a hundred years ago today, Christmas was already a children's holiday. Its economic impact was not overlooked, as Connecticut's own A.C. Gilbert went to Washington, D.C., in 1917 to make sure his toy company could continue to produce Erector Sets for Christmas and non-war-related materials. My father told me that story long before Hollywood created the Christmas movie about the man who saved Christmas. My father played with Erector Sets throughout his childhood, and a large working crane he constructed remains intact at his house. He also played with electric trains, a childhood staple of a hundred years ago.

"A hundred years ago" will always be a saying that we use it because it signifies a significant amount of time. My younger granddaughters will be in elementary school for the one hundredth anniversary of the Great Depression. How will that be so different from their lifestyle? They will be able to look at the date and know that the birth of their great-grandfather was also a hundred years ago. What will they think? Will they be amazed at how much has changed and how much has stayed the same?

## CRUISIN' ON MAIN: AN EVENT STEEPED IN TOWN TRADITION AND CUSTOM

"Look at that car!" One granddaughter draws my attention in one direction while the other pulls me directly opposite of the first. "It's blue. I love the blue car." My wife demands my eyes somewhere else.

Yes, it's "Cruisin' on Main" time once more. The nearly twenty-year-old event that fills Main Street with over one thousand classic and competition vehicles serves as a magnet for adults and children of all ages. The event was started in 2001 as a way to remember the Thursday evening cruising and shopping along Main Street. Thursday marked payday at the Cheney Silk Mills, which was the leading employer in Manchester for many years. Stores traditionally stayed open late that evening, a tradition that lasted into this generation.

Cars have always been a draw in Manchester. The Old Manchester Museum has photographs of vehicles from the early 1900s on. In fact, Manchester has seen horseless carriages on its streets since Christopher Spencer created his steam-powered vehicle in the 1860s. Spencer, a Manchester native, is one of the most unsung inventors in America. His work—not only at the Cheney Mills, but also later in his own endeavors— changed life in America. His vehicle transported him weekly around town and to Hartford and even Boston to check on his various enterprises.

After hearing from other residents and drawing on my childhood, this travel along the town streets has long been a family and young-adult rite of passage. To this day, families filter through town during the holidays, looking at home decorations. At one point in time, shopping trips were standard weekend car excursions. Church services and other social gatherings featured the family auto after the Second World War.

Cars lined Main Street, even in early 1920s Manchester. *Postcard from the author's collection.*

As automobiles became more prevalent, young adults started cruising Main Street on Thursdays and during the weekends. One such young man, who is now in his seventies, told me that he loved driving the "stem" from Hartford Road, up Main Street, to the round-a-bout on Center Street and back down Main Street. "You would drive up one side and circle around without a stop getting in your way," he said. The town removed Center Street's round-a-bout in the 1980s, and the center became the traffic light affair we know now.

Besides cruising Main Street, young men also found time to visit the Parkade Shopping Center and even the old Caldor's parking lot during their weekend activities. Now, we see the same adolescent rite of passage as young people walk around the mall.

The Cruisin' on Main event signals the end of the summer season for most students. It also marks the start of the shopping season, from the old sidewalk sales, when the stores lined Main Street with merchandise, to the pleasant environment of the spectacular holiday displays.

## *Afterword*

The first antique car show on Manchester's Main Street was hosted by Carter Chevrolet, which was located at the corner of Main and Charter Oak Street. That dealer had been located there since the 1930s and was an institution in the town. In the 2010s, the dealership moved to what is called the Flats (Tolland Turnpike along the Vernon border), and a pharmacy was constructed on the corner.

When I first moved back to Manchester, I was asked to speak about writing and to tell a story at the history society's annual dinner. The following is the story I told—of course, what else would it be but an automobile story?

# WITH A GRAIN OF SALT: THE CAR STORY

With Carter Chevrolet moving off Main Street, I remembered my aunt Henie's story of when my grandfather purchased his first car. Yes, it was a Ford Model T. He purchased it from Dillon Ford, another primary car dealer when I was growing up in town. She noted that he drove it down Center Street to the large brick house he had built to show off his building skills to potential clients. The house, now red once again, still stands on Center Street, near the newly constructed Community Health Resources (CHR) facility.

According to my aunt, he drove down the street, beeping the horn of the vehicle so that his family could see him come past, and they did. Dropping whatever they had been doing inside the house, they came outside to see what the noise was. They stood on the brick front porch and watched him proudly drive past, turn right onto Perkins Street and disappear from view. He soon returned back to Center Street by following the streets behind their house around in a circle. Once again, he laid on the horn, announcing his arrival, and once again, the children came out on the porch to wave their approval. Grandfather did this over and over, Henie confirmed, until he had run out of gas. It seemed that the salesman had forgotten to demonstrate the brake.

Now, I took this story with a grain of salt because I just could not see how a salesman could have forgotten to demonstrate the brake. I could not see how my grandfather could have traveled up Main Street from the Dillon Ford, located across from the hospital, through the center of town and onto Center Street without having to brake. So, the story sat in my head until one winter, when I slipped on ice, placing my standard transmission truck into a small hole in my driveway. My wife refused to help, noting that she had never learned to drive a standard. I boasted that anyone could drive the truck if they tried. My young teenage son was eager to demonstrate.

I placed him in the driver seat and showed him the clutch and the gas pedal. Reviewing that he needed only to pull off the clutch and tap the gas when I signaled, I headed to the front of the truck. Reaching the front, I looked into the windshield and nodded. My son smiled and nodded in acceptance of the responsibility. I called out "One, two, three," and pushed. My dutiful son popped the clutch and hit the gas, and the truck pulled backward. My push jumped it out of the hole, and I looked up triumphantly. "You can stop the truck now," I said, and my son shook his head as the vehicle continued rolling away. "Hit the break," I called, and he shrugged his shoulders in a replay. I had forgotten to show him how to use the brake. Fortunately, my son had only touched the gas, as instructed, and the truck rolled safely to a stop, inches from the garage. I knew then that my aunt's story was real.

The second point of doubt ended when I researched to find that Dillon Ford had not always been near the American Legion Hall on Main Street. At the time my grandfather purchased his Model T, it was on Center Street, across from a property my grandfather owned. My father claimed that my grandfather had tried to purchase the properties around this Center Street land. My Grandfather hoped to sell it to Dillon Ford so that he could build the new showroom for the car dealer. That transaction did not come about because one adjacent owner refused. The Ford dealer eventually left Center Street and became a town institution on Main Street. With this new knowledge, I realized that my grandfather could have coasted down the street to his home, no breaks needed. He just would have had to downshift gears to slow the vehicle.

Now, another auto institution has left that street for the Flats. What do you recall about Manchester's history?

## Remembering When Shopping Was More of an Adventure

Amazon announced that it would release a paper toy catalog this year (2019). I can already see my granddaughters fighting over who gets to look through it first and who gets which toy. What is old becomes new again, as the vision in my head recalls the times I held a vigil over the mail for the Sears or J.C. Penny toy catalogs. The big difference between these and Amazon's new approach is that my granddaughters will not be able to go to the store and hold the actual toy. They will only glimpse the desired item as it sparkles and shines in the glow of their parent's computer or cell phone screens.

Holiday shopping in Manchester has evolved from the early citizen's food and spirit purchases at the local general store to the highly specific computer selection of today. Remember when holiday shopping did not involve electricity and a flat screen but called for us to bundle in our winter coats, hats and gloves, crawl into the car and travel? Some journeyed to G. Fox of Hartford, but most stayed right here in Manchester.

First, we ventured to Main Street. There, Fairway and House & Hales drew in the parents for sophisticated items. Walkins called our attention to furniture that would last generations. Marlow's provided toys and practical household items for everyone if they could get past the endless cigar ash of the older Mr. Marlow. Treasures could be found in that five-and-dime if you knew where to look, and if you didn't, you could ask George, as he had the entire inventory and every item's location memorized.

Like a scene from *A Christmas Story*, for decades, Manchester's Main Street was all decorated with festive streetlights, a manger scene in Center Park and store displays. A dear friend of mine remembered that "you could travel Main Street and buy all your Christmas gifts for under five dollars." His special gift was a few White Owl cigars for his grandfather at Arthur's Drugstore. My wife recalled that Manchester Savings Bank had a Christmas Club where you placed fifty cents in an account every week all year. The bank kicked in a bonus interest rate, which came in during the holiday shopping season. With this fortune, my wife would bring endless joy to her family, especially her grandfather through his Aqua Velva and her Charlie perfume.

As Manchester grew, so did the shopping centers. The Parkade on Broad Street offered Kings, Bradlees and Grants to rival Marlow's and other Main Street stores. Here, dolls walked and talked, and Tommy guns were twist-tied to open cardboard boxes so customers could pull the triggers and make them rattle, becoming John Wayne. Convenient parking replaced the carol singers and the Thursday night gatherings on Main Street. Novelty stores that focused on books, electronics, appliances, clothing and more drew families to the new retail center. The winter elements still enhanced residents' enjoyment of venturing from one store to another. The merchants knew this, and several would offer hot cocoa or cider from the Bolton Cider Mill to the people who ventured into the night. Then, there was Kings—

before it moved to the Parkade—in the "gray" Cheney Mill building, which is now the site of apartments. And what would shopping be without a stop at Caldor's in Buckland?

All of these department stores are now history, but their replacements have roosted in the mall. Sears, Walmart and J.C. Penny brought Christmas shopping out of the elements and into the heated comfort of a large covered building. Decorations and piped-in music mesmerized shoppers into a holiday spirit, where frozen noses and numb ears never played a part.

So, my granddaughters will be fighting over the toy catalog. Will they ever know the joy of sweet hot cocoa mixed with the smell of a fresh evergreen tree tied to the roof of dad's car as they speed home from a family outing with Santa Claus and carol singers?

# Little Bits and Pieces of History Can Turn Up Anywhere, Anytime

People have notified me not only when I have made a mistake but also to help further my knowledge of Manchester history. Just the other Saturday, when I was at the Old Manchester Museum, a man came in with pictures and a copy of one of these columns. He pulled out the early 1900s picture of the Manchester Military Band. It was similar to one I had used to identify my grandfather and his cornet. The visitor to the museum explained that his grandfather had also been a cornet player and was a member of the Manchester Military Band. He pointed out a musician in the picture he brought, as well as family pictures that showed the same man.

This cornet player, Frank Schiebel, had come to Manchester from St. Polten, Austria. Settling in Manchester, he purchased a large piece of land on Adams Street, which became the family gathering place. Many relatives built houses near his home, creating St. John Street, and that area became populated Manchester with residents and continues to the present day.

Several people have talked to me about their positions at the Cheney Mills and Pioneer Parachute. It was interesting to hear that a future airborne soldier worked at Pioneer while in high school before joining the United States Marine Airborne Corps. Little bits and pieces of information like this help bring the history of the community alive. We encourage you to share this information whenever possible with myself and other members of the historical society.

## 5

# Town Divided

## THE CHENEY FAMILY WAS THE FABRIC THAT HELD MANCHESTER TOGETHER FOR DECADES

"Grandpa, what's a Cheney?" my youngest granddaughter asked, and I knew it was time to tell her of the town's matriarchal family.

Few buildings outside of the mill complex display the Cheney name. It has become easy to overlook the nature and generosity of the family that dominated Manchester life for three generations from the mid-1800s to around 1960. The Cheney brothers opened their silk mill in the 1830s and watched it grow into the nation's largest silk mill. From a handful of employees to over four thousand at its height, the company provided a stable financial base for Manchester.

The family's dominance can still be seen on a drive past the massive brick mill complex off of Hartford Road. The mansions alongside the same road hint at the wealth of the family. But what is hidden or almost forgotten are the gifts the Cheney family gave to the town.

Education square is still visible (Bennet Academy complex). The four large brick classroom buildings were a gift from the Cheneys to the town after the Ninth District fire destroyed the South End's school. The old Manchester High School (Bennet Apartments) had been given to the city from the family a few years earlier than the rest of the complex. A past historical society president noted that the reservoirs that today provide water

This view shows the Cheney Mills in the early 1900s. *Postcard from the author's collection.*

to the town were the greatest legacy of the Cheneys. These abundant water supplies were initially designed to service the mills and, at a modest fee, the houses around southern Manchester. They were sold to the town for one dollar in the 1930s. For years, churches throughout the South End were provided with funding from the Cheney family for their construction and annual budgets. Needleless to say, the Mary Cheney Library, which is the only public building that bears the family name, was a gift from the family. The hall of records (now the probate court) and the Central Memorial and Center Springs Parks came from the Cheneys as well. A golf course, which was first located at what is now the high school and was then moved to the country club, was also a family donation.

Anonymous gifts from the family were also common, not just to residents, but also to organizations like the hospital and Army and Navy Club, as well as to the town itself. During the Great Depression, a guarantee from the family allowed the city to borrow budget money from a Boston bank, preventing the city from going bankrupt. The Cheney family members also did their fair share of town officiating. Several town committees, especially the board of selectmen and the board of education, had a Cheney as a member.

But above all else, the Cheney family created an atmosphere of family and unity in the town. Over the years, they were the glue that many families needed for their economic security. They operated under the principle that everyone at Cheney Mills should progress as far as they want. The family promoted a robust education system that provided a well-rounded art, business and college-oriented curriculum. Finally, when the mills did close, the workforce of Manchester was not unprepared. Most of the residents found work with Pratt and Whitney or other manufacturers around the area. They were not burdened with one set of skills that they could not transfer, but they utilized the adaptable skills they learned at Cheney Mills.

The Cheneys even influenced the town's shopping routines. Older residents will recall that, on Thursday evenings, all the stores in town stayed open late, and families gathered on Main Street. This activity occurred because Cheney Mills paid its workers on Thursday instead of Friday.

## *Afterword*

This article sparked some resistance from a peer who thought I was promoting the old Cheney myth. But in reality, that myth was based on fact. Having traveled across this country and having lived in several other old mill towns, I saw what the Cheneys gave Manchester is immeasurable. As a candidate for my master's degree, I prepared a study comparing Manchester to Willimantic, Connecticut. Both were textile mill towns, but when the old mills closed, Willimantic suffered, while Manchester remained strong. The education system in each city reflected the attitudes of the mill owners. Windham had a three-Rs primary curriculum, with the workers being educated in only the skills they needed for their specific jobs at the mill. Under the guidance of the Cheney-dominated board of education, Manchester offered a curriculum that was designed to take a worker as far as they wanted to go.

# TOWN'S EIGHTH DISTRICT HISTORY GOES BACK MORE THAN A CENTURY

"Grandpa, what does it mean 'Eighth District' on that building sign?" my granddaughter asked about the office building on Main Street. "It's a separate fire district," I answered, not sure how to explain that there was an independent district within Manchester. The North End area, called the Eighth District, maintains some self-regulated functions from the rest of the town. How did this happen?

Depot Square was the commercial section of the old North End and later the Eighth District. *Postcard from the author's collection.*

Like many I know, I also thought the Eighth District was as old as the town, but in reality, the Eighth Utilities District is just a little over one hundred years old. I discovered this fact in a 1978 report composed by David McQuade. He had researched the Eighth District at a time when issues arose about the district's expansion.

The 1915 General Assembly Special Act 299 established the Eighth School and Utilities District. This act allowed residents to raise taxes to maintain a fire department, sanitary system and garbage disposal unit and to oversee the educational system. Later, the assembly authorized the district to expand its area if the majority of the additional area landowners approved through a vote. The district's name was also changed to the Eighth Utilities District.

Like many other towns in the state, Manchester started as a number of small communities that united under a central government as needs and financial obligations increased. Manchester had several "villages" and district areas as a young entity, including Lydallville, Buckland, Hillardville, the Green and Cheneyville. These small outposts generally grew up around a tavern, general store and small mill or farming enterprise. As time drew them together, centrally located churches and town meeting halls provided a united community. This consolidation became common as roads and travel allowed for better connections. For years, district post offices and schools maintained their individual identities. Manchester would centralize its post offices in the 1930s and 1940s. Its schools united under one district after the 1920s.

In the early history of the town, Unionville, which became the North End, dominated the population and employment of Manchester. The North End hosted several commercial mills, which produced cloth, paper and soap. It also maintained its school. Today's Robertson was the successor of the Unionville School, which was located near the current board of education building. The Hartford-to-Providence train constructed its stations in Buckland and at the north end of Main Street. These stations of the 1850s showed that the rest of the world considered Manchester's North End the commercial hub of the community. But the area's mills began to shut down or move in the late 1800s, shifting the employment and political center of Manchester to the South End, which was dominated by the Cheney Mills and the Cheney family.

When the debate for a new town hall was waged, the Cheney family's gift of land at the center of town spun the town's political power even farther south. Many local historians note that this shift left a bad taste in the mouths of the North End's residents. Even the location of the high school could not be shared. It was originally a part of the Cheney-run Ninth District. The 1910 construction of the large brick building on Main Street only added salt to the wound. A final blow came in the 1880s, when Cheney Mills provided a sewer and water system for the South End at almost no cost. Residents of the North End, however, did not get to share in this system. Even after health officials cited a desperate need for a new sewer system to replace the North End's ill-kept private cesspools, the North Enders could not get support from the town to help pay the construction costs. The political power and purse strings were kept in the hands of the residents of the other areas of Manchester.

Closed out of this avenue for financing, the North Enders approached the state. The assembly took up the cause and authorized the Eighth District's creation, making it a small community within the town. Time has left only the fire department and some building oversight that is still in the hands of the independent governing body.

## *Afterword*

This column sparked several suggestions that the Eighth District was older than the state's authorization of its creation. The residents wanted to let me know that the volunteer fire department still operated in the section of the town that dated back to the 1880s. They also wanted me to include the fact that the district was much more than a fire department; it still had utility oversight in the area. The feelings expressed suggested that the residents wished for readers to feel that the district functioned as a separate community dating back to the Unionville heydays of the 1860s. The issue with this is that, during these days, tax money ran the entire town of Manchester, not just the district itself.

# 6
# *Manufacturers*

## PITKIN GLASSWORKS RUINS ARE EVIDENCE OF MANCHESTER'S PAST ECONOMIC ROYALTY

Walking along Parker and Putnam Streets, my granddaughter stopped and asked me, "How big was the castle? The ruins are huge." I was puzzled and then recalled that the remains of the Pitkin Glassworks were on the corner of the street. In the mind of a three-year-old, the massive stone structure could be confused with those of a ruined English castle. There are even members of the Pitkin Glassworks Society who call the ruins "the abbey," a hint at how it compares to Elizabethan abbey ruins of England.

In reality, the site is the location of the first large-scale manufacturing outfit in Manchester. Operating from just after the American Revolution to the 1830s, the Pitkin Glassworks produced some of the most exquisite glassware of the period. It provided the town with its first significant family and place in the history of the nation. Over the years, other Manchester manufacturers and families may have overshadowed the accomplishments of the Pitkins, but their achievements should not be forgotten. The glassworks bridged the gap between Manchester's creation as an East Hartford break (Orford Parish) to its creation as the independent township of Manchester. The Pitkin family played a significant role in the creation of the town, both financially and culturally.

The ruins of the Pitkin Glass Works. Early American glass bottles that were blown here were used to ship various materials as far as the West Indies and back. *Author's photograph.*

The glasswork's founder, Richard Pitkin, was sent back from the battlefield by General George Washington himself to produce and provide gun powder for the Patriot army. His efforts were rewarded with a monopoly in manufacturing glass in Connecticut for twenty-four years. This means he did not have any competition from any other factories in the state.

Pitkin's factory employed many local workers, whose houses dotted the area around Porter, Pitkin and Parker Street. One example of such a shelter is still located on Porter Street across from the end of Pitkin Street. Richard's own house still stands on Porter Street near the factory and dates back to 1788.

Besides their remarkable glassware, which was estimated to be worth thousands of dollars in today's money, the Pitkins also had a monopoly on producing snuff. This tobacco-oriented product was very fashionable throughout the 1830s.

During its heyday, the glasswork's furnaces burned twenty-four hours a day and were operated by workers who pulled twelve-hour shifts. The firewood was produced locally, but the Pitkins imported sand from New

Jersey; it was transported to the area by wagon from a docked barge in East Hartford. When the costs of raw material increased beyond profitability, the factory closed.

During the Revolutionary War, Dorothy Pitkin etched her place in Manchester's folklore. Her meals provided nutrition to the men who responded to the Lexington-Concord alarm that signaled the first battle of the war. Later, she also served a large meal to the French troops who were on their way to Yorktown, the final major battle of the war. The site of these suppers has been in dispute, but they occurred near the glasswork's ruins.

Today, you can only see two of the outside walls of the glassworks, which were constructed of Bolton quarry granite. The building's interior and its other walls are a mystery to historians and visitors alike. There is no actual painting of the factory from its days of operations. There is no sketch or picture of the factory with its roof. The Pitkin Glassworks Society is currently asking architecture engineers to create a rendition of how the building may have looked based on the walls and stonework that remain. Meanwhile, we get to look at the site in wonder not about the knights who lived there, as my granddaughters do, but about the Manchester families whose artistic work still demands respect among the glass collectors of the world.

## *Afterword*

The Pitkin Glass Works Committee's efforts to develop a drawing of the operating factory have uncovered this late 1700s Boston newspaper article. It is a reprinting of a letter from an East Hartford "gentleman" to a Boston glassworks facility looking for skilled glass workers.

> *The prefects we have in bringing the manufacture of window glass to great perfection in this state are evident to everyone who wishes to promote so useful an undertaking. Here are some few people that never wish to have glass or any other articles manufactured in the state, but their influence with us is not great. The gentlemen that are concerned in this useful business are men of much wealth and highly spirited in their undertakings and have no doubt, but they can make glass of equal quality with any imported from Europe, and much cheaper. The wood in this state is large and very plenty. The materials for the glass is also plenty and can be had on reasonable terms. They have already a capital of 14,000 pounds and will increase it to 20,000 pounds.*

*Their manufacturing house is built with stone, is four stories high, and wide enough to admit [wagons] of many lengths. Mr. Robert Hewes from Boston is chief artisan and superintends the works. His abilities are not confined to the glass manufacture alone, he is master of other [skills] equally as useful, and which will also meet with proper encouragement in due time.*

At a recent Pitkin Executive Council meeting, the president quoted a 1923 article from the *Hartford Courant*. This write up notes that the building was only three stories with a hexagon roof. Which write up is accurate? We will just have to wait for the architectural engineers.

## THE OTHER GLASSWORKS!

Did you know there was another glass manufacturer in Manchester other than Pitkin Glassworks? That information also came to me when the museum was visited by brothers who grew up on Mather Street. This other company, the Mather Glassworks, was located near Salter's Pond and the Lydall Paper Mill on Parker and Mather Streets. It was not as productive as Pitkin, but it still produced beautiful glassware and gun powder, according to Pitkin Glassworks president David Smith. It was this latter product that caused trouble—and the company's downfall.

It seems that the Mather Powder Mill blew up, and the people of the town were not very happy about it. They asked that the company move a little farther off the main road, which it did before blowing up again. Official records are scarce as to what happened to the Mather Mill. In one account, there was a fire at the mill and then it was later destroyed again by a hurricane. Either way, the mill disappeared into history.

The brothers who talked with me at the museum noted that they found small pieces of glass shards, the byproducts of the company around the pond. Growing up, they thought this glass came from Pitkin, unaware that another company ran a glassworks in town.

# The Cheney Brothers' Story
## Is One of Innovation and Dominance

"Grandpa, what's silk?" My youngest granddaughter asked the strangest question someone can ask, considering Manchester was once the largest silk producer in the nation—if not the world.

The Cheney Brothers Silk Mills operated from 1830 until the 1970s, producing all types of products, from raw silk to finished material. Cheney dominated the market for over a century. From scarves to parachutes, the silky fabric was all Manchester-made. It was a family-controlled business for three generations. The founding Cheney brothers started the company as a single Hop Brook mill in the 1830s. They watched it grow into the nation's largest silk mill. From a handful of employees to over four thousand at its height, the company provided a stable financial base for Manchester.

The original brothers who founded the mills were the children of Electa Woodbridge Cheney, who had given President Washington a cup of water. Her fame was overshadowed by her children, and they were overshadowed tenfold by their children. The Cheney brothers worked hard to develop a productive mill and the machines necessary to produce silk from the worms that were imported to Manchester from China. They had also been

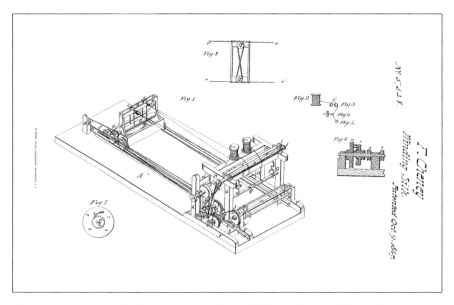

Silk weaving machine developed by Frank Cheney. His inventive mind allowed the company to prosper. *Image courtesy of USPO.*

This banner of Cheney Silk is part of the society's exhibit on internationally famous manufacturers. *Courtesy of the Manchester Historical Society.*

part of an effort to grow mulberry trees to feed the silkworms; however, that effort fell victim to a genetic disease, though Manchester still hosts some mulberry trees.

The production side of the business prospered under the brothers' guidance. It was in interventions and machinery development that the Cheneys found cost-saving results and the efficiency needed to become a leading manufacturer. Frank Cheney and his older brother Rush were instrumental in the development or modification of existing machines that allowed for the spinning and weaving of silk from the worm. But more importantly, the brothers developed a method to reclaim broken silk thread. This process picked up the scrap silk strands and made them into profitable material. The Cheneys' inventions and patents brought in additional revenue to the mills as other manufacturers tried to compete against them.

Besides silk, the brothers in the third generation tried to expand into nylon and other man-made materials. Still, their hearts were not into these ventures.

Helping the brothers achieve their early success were tariffs, which helped place imported silk at a higher cost, but their quality held onto the market. Cheney silk would win some of the most prestigious honors in the industry for its quality. This global dominance in the market required the Cheney brothers to have offices in Hartford, New York, California, London and China.

## Afterword

What sparks a lot of conversation is the confusion many people have concerning the leadership at Cheney Brothers. The family maintained a tight grip on the company for three generations. The fact that many of the brothers had the same name has led to the continual attribution of significant accomplishments to the wrong generations. For example, there were three Franks heavily involved in the running and innovation of the mills. The original Frank was the youngest of the original seven brothers, but his involvement happened in the mid-1860s; at the same time, Colonial Frank W. Cheney, a nephew, was taking the reins of power. Finally, Frank Jr., the son of the first Frank, came to power as Frank W. was beginning to divest himself from the company. The achievements of the three are often mixed together.

# YOUR MANCHESTER: LAWSUITS DOOMED MANCHESTER'S CHANCE FOR LIGHTBULB FAME

My students have been doing their capstone presentations, and one of the most popular topics has been the conversion of our cars from gas to electricity. But that topic has been studied for well over one hundred years in this state. Just over one hundred years ago, Hartford was the center of the car industry, with Pope Hartford leading the way in production. But why do we forget this fact?

A lawsuit forced Albert Pope of Hartford to give up his electrically powered vehicle kingdom to the Ford gas-oriented vehicles. The court ruled that Pope's design was a violation of Ford's patents. The Hartford resident's dream of battery-operated cars became a fading mirage. Pope had argued with his developers that people, especially female drivers, would rather maintain an electric vehicle, which they could handle without getting their hands dirty with oil and grease. He had been the developer of the electric tramcars and buses found throughout the nation at the time. His electric cars were a big success until Ford joined with Rockefeller to place a gas station on just about every corner.

Another lawsuit provided Connecticut resident Alexander Graham Bell the exclusive rights to the telephone. This suit cut out other inventors who had been working on similar developments in communications simultaneously with Bell. Bell went on to have a history textbook–worthy career.

In Manchester, a similar court case concerned a resident's rights to dynamo manufacturing. This time, it was the Mather Electric Company that came up short in its efforts to maintain patent rights, and its foe was Thomas Edison. Mather Electric started in 1883 as a dynamo manufacturer. Eventually, it moved to a large brick factory on Hilliard Street, now the Time Machine. By 1888, over one hundred people were working for Mather, and the company looked toward changing its focus to lightbulb production to light the world.

Obtaining the rights to the Perkins bulb patent, the company created a branch called the Perkins Electric Light Company, and it sank a large amount of its capital into the project. The Perkins Company was one of several small factory bulbs found throughout the country at this time until Edison's lawyers saw them as competition. Edison took the company to court, and he won his lawsuit, forcing Mather to stop making the bulb.

However, Mather was not discouraged, and he put his remaining money behind another bulb. This one was patented by an inventor named Waring.

This factory sheltered both the Mather Company and Bon Ami Soap. *Author's photograph.*

Again, Edison sued the Manchester company and won. This second lawsuit may have been followed by a third, as Mather had yet another bulb design, but the capital was not available. Mather declared bankruptcy, and the chance for Manchester to become the electrical bulb kingdom faded into dark—as did Hartford's chance to be the automobile center of the universe.

# MANCHESTER WAS ONCE A LEADER IN SOAP MAKING

Bon Ami was a common sight in American homes. *Author's photograph.*

"Why is there a baby chick picture in the history book?" my granddaughter asked as she looked through the local history books I have in my office. Throughout several of these publications, there is the "Bon Ami Chick" picture, as it has a connection to Manchester. Still producing today, the Bon Ami soap factory is in New Jersey. Yet, initially, the soap was made right here in Manchester. In fact, Manchester almost became the soap kingdom of the nation. Imagine that; Manchester almost had the top two soap manufactures in the nation, as well as the Cheney Silk Mills.

Bon Ami started when two brothers brought the J.T. Robertson Soap Company from Glastonbury and set up shop in Unionville. They had been looking for a location where they could afford to expand their production of soap. They found the vacant Mather Electric factory on Hilliard Street; it was in just the right spot for the growth and further development of their commercial detergents.

Once they were established in the town, they centered the company's attention on the development of a nonabrasive cleaner that would allow you to clean objects without producing streaks and scratches. It first came to the market in cake form in 1886. The brothers used feldspar as the central ingredient and refused to add perfumes or other additives, allowing the company to promote its product as a natural way of cleaning without scratching.

The name Bon Ami means "good friend" in French, and the company soon became an international success.

The baby chick with the cracked eggshell was the brand's promotional symbol to show how safe and gentle the product was. To further enhance this point, they added the wording, "Hasn't Scratched Yet," indicating that the chick, fresh from hatching, does not scratch for food, and Bon Ami soap does not scratch either. This promotional masterpiece was first presented to the general public in the late 1800s, after the company was well entrenched in Manchester. This trademark, registered in 1892, is one of the oldest registered trademarks in the nation.

Bon Ami switched to a powder cleanser in 1913, and the company continued to produce its powder soap and other products in town until after the Second World War. Older residents have told me that they can still remember the smell of the soap whenever they pass through the North End. In 1971, the company was acquired by the Faultless Starch Company, ending the company's Manchester connection.

In a strange bit of fate, the J.B. Williams Company of Glastonbury, Connecticut, actually started here. J.B. Williams was the owner of Manchester's Green's General Store in the early 1800s. He spent time behind the shop, which still stands today, perfecting his shaving soap. He also began selling it from this location—first locally, then nationally. When his demand required a larger production capacity, he looked around for an old mill he could afford. His financial backers found a mill in Glastonbury. From there, his product became the leading shaving soap across the nation and the world. He continued to expand in Glastonbury not only his Williams shaving soap production but also his aftershave, Aqua Velva. Both products are still being produced today under the same names by a company headquartered in France, and they are manufactured in New Jersey.

How close we were to having the cleanest—or soapiest—town in the country.

# OLD MILL ON THE GREEN WAS BIG IN THE LONG JOHN BUSINESS

"Itchy long johns and woolen shirts." That is what most people think about when they picture a Maine lumberjack or a resident of New England from the early 1900s. Those itchy long johns most likely came from right here in Manchester.

The Green section of Manchester has been the home of a large wood-and-brick mill building since the mid-1800s. The complex itself has been the home of many businesses aside from the knitting manufacturer. In my lifetime, it has been a furniture store, print shop, a shoe store (the place I had my first job outside of my father's office) and a used bookstore—just to mention a few. Recently purchased, there is a plan to convert the site into senior apartments.

The current building was originally constructed in 1851 as the home of the Pacific Cotton Mill; it was meant to replace another mill that had been destroyed by a fire in the same location. A water wheel initially provided power for the mill. It was located inside the building, as the foundation was built

MANCHESTER GREEN AND GLASTONBURY KNITTING CO., SO, MANCHESTER, CONN.

The Glastonbury Mill produced long johns at the Green. *Postcard from the author's collection.*

alongside a stream that meandered through the Manchester Green area. This stream was later channeled by Aaron Cook to provide a water system for this section of town in the late 1800s and early 1900s. The Manchester Green water company disbanded after the town built the brick Green School, which is now a senior center, disrupting the water system's path.

Future Civil War general John Otis helped established the Pacific Cotton Company in Manchester. Eventually, he became a partner before he left in 1856 to start his business, Otis Manufacturing, in a mill along the Hop Brook, near today's Charter Oak Park. Under different leadership, the Pacific Company continued to produce cotton products at the Green, but bankruptcy and fire ended production in the late 1800s. For a brief time, the Seamless Hosiery Company operated there as well.

In 1890, the mill became the Glastonbury Knitting Company, which was owned by Addison Clark of Glastonbury. After Clark's death, Hewitt Coburn bought the mill. His partner and vice president, Walter Coburn, lived at the Green and made the local community a focus of his attention. Coburn Road runs off East Middle Turnpike, just west of the Green, forever linking his name to the town.

Men's long johns became the mill's chief product, as it produced over 250,000 pairs of the flat-knit, spring-needle woolen underwear a year. By

1920, more than one hundred employees worked at the mill, producing the highest-quality stock. Historian William Buckley noted that his father was one of these employees.

Buckley wrote that the Great Depression, along with the owner's unwillingness to change with the times by producing other products, helped slow the weaving machines in the mills. By 1930, the company was in sharp decline, and it was out of business by 1932. From this point forward, the building was never an active mill again. It became the host of a wide variety of retail and small businesses, including a fitness center, a printer and even a barbershop.

# 7

# *Famous Inventions*

## MANCHESTER INVENTOR WAS DEVOTED TO IMPROVING WASHING MACHINES

"What's that?" my youngest grandchild asked as she looked at a white tub washing machine with an attached silver-top wringer. The device, which dates from the 1940s, lives in my father's barn. It has been in the barn for as long as I can remember. My father had a habit of hanging on to items that "could be useful" sometime down the line. I have no clue where this particular machine came from; it may have been my grandmother's, but it was there, and it was a great conversation piece for my granddaughters.

During the 1930s and 1940s, when machines like this one were found in homes, clothes were placed in the round tub section at the bottom and washed—generally as they are in today's devices. The operator then had to remove the wet items and either hand-crank them through the wringer or, like this model, allow a small electric motor to pull the clothes through the wringer.

The washing machine has made wearing clothes utterly different than it was even one hundred years ago. Before the washing machine, it was common for a person to wear the same clothes several days in a row. It was also common for people to have only one special suit of clothing for special days, including every Sunday. Clothes lasted longer because they did not endure the wear brought about by regular washing.

This 1940s washing machine wringer was a modification of a Manchester idea. *Author's photograph.*

Manchester's connection to the clothes washing industry is more interesting than you may think. Besides the fact that washing soap was a significant product of the Orford Soap Company (Bon Ami), Manchester was also involved in the development of the washing machine itself.

John H. Malone of south Manchester held a patent on "improvements pertaining to washing-machines and wringing-machines" back in 1875. His patented devise, as presented in the official request, focused on an improvement in the wringer. The improvement, the patent reads, redesigned the rotary roll, which consisted of a series of stationary rubbers pressing on the lower roll. Instead, Malone designed a system of multiple, spring-controlled rubber-headed pressure feet situated in the top roller. When a piece of cloth entered the wringer, the top roller would match the contour of the material, allowing for a better universal wringing than a single-pressure roller provided across different cloth thicknesses. Malone also felt that his design would help prevent jamming.

Malone explained it this way on his patent request:

> *The lower ends of the rubbers are rounded. The making of these rubbers in a separate series maintains an equal or nearly equal pressure on the clothes*

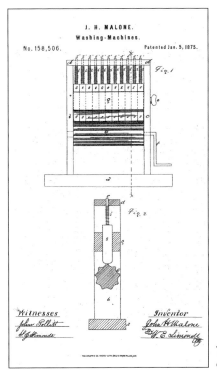

These washing machine wringer plans were developed in Manchester. *Image courtesy of USPO.*

*passed through the machine along the whole length of the roll, while if they were made all in one piece, this would not be so.*

*It being an essential feature of my invention to have a series of rubbers covering the length of the roll, each rising and falling independently of the others, so that if the cloth passing through the machine is thicker at some one point than at the other points, only the rubber or rubbers immediately overlying the point of greater thickness is raised to an extra height, leaving the other rubbers undisturbed in their action upon the cloth where it is of less thickness.*

*The roll and rubbers are, by preference, made of metal coated with zinc or tin so as not to be rusted by the water, but any proper material may be used.*

What happened to this mechanically minded resident?

Malone lived in South Manchester at the time of his patent, but he then moved out of town. His name is unlisted in the early town directories (later 1880s) that can be found at the Manchester Historical Society. Other inventions by this Manchester native also do not appear when you search the patent office records. The closest patent to the 1875 date is for a tank-heater by a John Malone of Nebraska in 1917.

# PIZZA SHOP HAS MUCH DEEPER HISTORY

"It's just a pizza place," my granddaughter said as we walked out of the building that houses Woodbridge Pizza at 489 East Middle Turnpike on the Green. It's just a pizza shop now, but the location has a history that dominated Manchester lore and garnered national fame. My granddaughter looked at me and asked, "Do buildings have history too?" I smiled and nodded.

When I was younger, the restaurant was there, but it was under a different name. The front door of the existing structure has welcomed visitors for over one hundred years. The building has served not only as a restaurant, but also as a general store and post office. Throughout the town's history, pictures of the building show the little changes that have come and gone from the building's facade.

The site was the second post office for the town of Manchester. The letterboxes and wooden postmaster's work area are on display at the Old Manchester Museum. The first post office was across the street in the Woodbridge Tavern. It was moved to this location by postmaster Wells Woodbridge, a brother of the tavern owner and the farmer who ran the Woodbridge Farm. At the time, the area was called Orford Parish but was known Manchester by 1820. The museum display consists of small glass-and-metal-door mailboxes and the outgoing mail slot that was used by residents to correspond with relatives and businesses across the country. It harkens back to a time when people gathered at the general store to share national and state news and local gossip.

What I picture more when I look at the building and the postmaster's workbench is the history that has passed over this workstation. This bench received letters from across the nation, including official U.S. patent office paperwork on items that changed the world, not just Manchester.

The Green area of the town was the original business center of Manchester. Among the residents were innovative Connecticut Yankees and blacksmiths who had to find solutions to prosper in the rock-infested soil of Connecticut. The area boasted several carriage shops, as well as the blacksmith shop of Benjamin Lyman. This jack of all trades developed various farming tools to handle the environment, including metal plows and cutting edges. The U.S. patent office was not a stranger to his correspondence. Lyman's successor, Aaron Cook Jr., continued to develop farming instruments in the same shop at the Green, but his influence reached out to Frank Holland. This educator at the Green School teamed with Cook to tackle a school-oriented problem. Holland's three patents

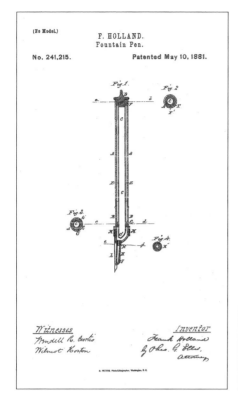

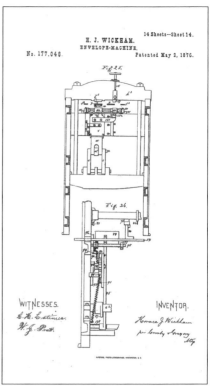

*Left*: These fountain pen plans are just some examples of so many inventions that were created here in Manchester. *Image courtesy of USPO.*

*Right*: The envelope machine was just one of over forty patents that were held by the Wickham father-son team of Manchester. *Image courtesy of USPO.*

from the 1880s focused on pens that held and released ink on demand (what we call a fountain pen today). His work formed the basic design for the Waterman premier pen.

Another Manchester Green inventor, Horace Wickman, developed machines that folded paper into envelopes. This invention was another daily object with patent papers that traveled through the Manchester Green Post Office. His neighbor Maro Chapman helped him sell his products, creating the business empire of Plimpton Manufacturing, which was centered in Hartford. Wickham held over twenty-two patents—from envelope machines to wrappers.

Even earlier, this pizza building's location saw the development of yet another product that is still used around the world daily. A clerk and short-time store owner, J.B. Williams, spent his spare time in Manchester perfecting a formula for shaving soap. Eventually, his soap brought in enough money to mass-produce it, and Williams moved his production to a Glastonbury mill. J.B. Williams's shaving soaps came to dominate the market, as did his aftershave lotion, Aqua Velva.

"So, is it just a pizza shop or a historical landmark?" My granddaughter could not answer.

## MANCHESTER'S MOST LEGENDARY PERSON

"Are there any people who were legends in this town?" My granddaughter asked the other day. "Being a legend depends on what you consider amazing," I responded. "And having legends told about a person depends on what you consider the difference between fact and storytelling." She gave me one of her looks, and I explained.

There are a lot of stories or legends centered around one of the most inventive minds that was ever born in Manchester, Christopher M. Spencer. According to legend, this gifted child tinkered with almost anything in the house and around the homestead.

One day, according to this legend, Frank Cheney, while visiting his friend Owen Spencer, found the place in an uproar. Cheney, himself a tinkerer and inventor of national renewal, asked what the issue was. Cheney was shown a pendulum drive clock in pieces on the table. It seemed that the young Christopher had wanted to see how the device operated. Cheney asked the boy, now that he had it apart, if he could put it back together. Without hesitation, Spencer did while Frank watched. Cheney immediately requested that the boy be at the mill the next morning for a position in the company repair shop.

How much of that story is true I'll leave to my granddaughter to research. What we do know is that Frank Cheney was good friends with Christopher's uncle Owen. We also know that Christopher was very interested in mechanical things from a young age, so his parents allowed him to live with his grandfather. The latter taught the boy how to use a lathe. Today, we would call him a boy genius. Spencer was a great Yankee tinkerer, and eventually, he was head of the repair shop at the Cheney Brothers Silk Mills. By the time the Manchester man died in 1922, over forty patents had carried his name.

These Spencer guns are part of a society display on one of Manchester's leading inventors. *Courtesy of the Manchester Historical Society.*

At fourteen, Spencer started his employment with Cheney. He learned the ins and outs of the various sewing machines used in the mills by repairing damaged and worn-out machines. After a year of working under Frank Cheney's tutorage, Christopher left Manchester to journeyman at mills in New York, Massachusetts and Connecticut, learning more and more about different types of manufacturing machines. His first patent came during this time. While working in the Willimantic Linen Company, he developed an automatic silk-winding machine. He eventually worked at Colts in Hartford, learning the process of gun manufacturing.

Finally, he returned to Manchester and his employment at Cheney Brothers in the late 1850s. A bit of mythology states that Spencer was sent out by Frank Cheney to the other mills to improve his machinery knowledge. Cheney knew the boy would return to help Cheney. The facts note that Cheney encouraged him to broaden his knowledge of machines and mechanical principals. In 1855, Spencer took over the operations at Cheney's Hartford Ribbon Mill. Besides his administrative and repair duties, he was given free run of the repair shop to tinker on whatever he wanted after the mill's machines had been fixed. And boy, did he tinker. Out of his free time came a steam-driven car. This vehicle was not the first of its kind in the world or even in America. From it, however, according to legend, came a whole new company that still touches us today, Traveler's Insurance.

Spencer had a habit of driving his steam vehicle from Manchester to Boston in the 1860s, and one day, he scared a horse and wagon. The incident caused an accident, and he was sued. His friends formed a company that would provide insurance against such claims as he traveled. This legend does not appear in the official history of the insurance company, but it could easily be inferred. Traveler's was officially started in 1863, around the same time Spencer was driving to Boston, as a joke between Hartford businessmen who asked how much would "$5,000 of insurance against accidental death on his way home" cost. The price was two cents, which the first businessman paid and the other kept when the first made it home safely. A company was born. What is fact, however, is that Spencer had an early policy with the Traveler's Insurance Company.

Another thing that Christopher developed while tinkering in Cheney's repair shop was a rifle—not a musket, as was standard at that time. It was a gun that could be loaded with seven rounds and fired one right after the other without priming or using a ramrod. The musket could fire around two to three bullets a minute, while Spencer's could click off twenty rounds or more a minute. By 1860, he had a patent on the repeater. He was even demonstrating it for the United States Army and Navy as the country entered the American Civil War. The Spencer repeating rifle was an instant success among frontline army officers and the Naval Department, but it was not popular with the Ordnance Department of the U.S. Army that was fighting the American Civil War. The general in charge thought a soldier might waste bullets if he was able to fire so many at once.

Once more, legend mixes with fact concerning Christopher Spencer. Unable to get the War Department to OK purchases and production of the weapon, the Cheney family arranged a meeting with President Lincoln himself. Bringing a Spencer Rifle to the White House, the Manchester resident managed to have the president test fire the rifle on the back lawn. Some accounts say Lincoln actually crossed to the mall and fired near the Washington Monument. Most accounts recall that Lincoln fired the weapon and hit a target near the bullseye five times. He handed the repeater over to

Spencer, who proceeded to demonstrate not only the weapon's accuracy, but also its speed. Lincoln was so impressed with the weapon that he ordered the War Department to purchase it. Most historians, however, question this last statement, as they can find little interference by Lincoln in any Ordnance Department orders concerning this weapon or any weapon.

At this time, the rifle actually had already seen action in the war. Cavalry units like the Michigan Brigade commanded by George Custer had used them to grand effect before and during the battle of Gettysburg. At Gettysburg, Spencer's rifle won high acclaim, as it was said a soldier could load on Sunday and fire all week. On the third day of the largest Civil War battle, the Confederates tried to end the actions by sending J.E.B. Stuart's army around the rear of the Union forces. Fortunately for the Union, General Custer's Michigan Brigade (which was smaller than an army) was in the path of Stuart's march.

Custer, a former cavalry officer, had seen the Spencer repeater's value in actions before Gettysburg. He made sure his troops carried the weapon. When Stuart's forces tried to sweep around the Union flank, they suddenly came up against Custer's units. The Union troopers put up such a volume of shot that they stopped the Confederates, opening the day for a victory.

This same intensity of bullets was evidenced against Custer some years later when he led his Seventh Cavalry into the Little Big Horn Valley. Then, it was the Native Americans who held the Spencer repeaters against Custer, and like at they did at Gettysburg, the Spencer rifles provided victory on the battlefield.

Manchester's Christopher Spencer should not be remembered for these two tinkered inventions, however. Let us honor him for something that affects all of our lives daily, a simple machine that he developed while not at Cheneys.

During the Civil War, the Cheney brothers helped Spencer finance a company that produced rifles. He also met other manufacturers, including Charles E. Billings. Through this contact, he learned the trade of drop forging. This process arranges hammers (small to large) to drop on metal, creating dies and other small metal pieces. Spencer helped with the development of metal lathes to produce small intricate parts for various machines. Spencer used this method to perfect devices to help build his weapons and other products. The Billings and Spencer Drop-Forging Tool and Die Company would continue for many years as a leading employer in the Hartford area.

Combining his knowledge of these skills, in the 1870s, Christopher Spencer created his screw machine. This device allowed him to mass-produce

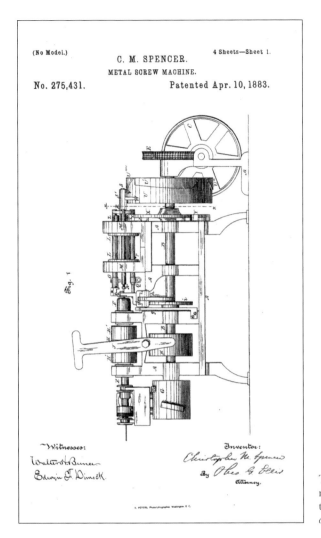

(No Model.)      4 Sheets—Sheet 1.

C. M. SPENCER.

METAL SCREW MACHINE.

No. 275,431.      Patented Apr. 10, 1883.

The Spencer screw machine helped create the world we know. *Image courtesy of USPO.*

threaded screws at a significant profit. Let's think. Which do we use more often each day, a rifle or something held together by metal screws? Spencer's Hartford Machine Screw Company was one of the leading manufactures in the central Connecticut area.

He later returned to manufacturing a peacetime repeating shotgun and experimented with various steam-driven cars before he died in 1922. After leaving Cheney's in the 1860s, most of his adult life was spent in Hartford and Windsor.

# 8

# *Nature's Gifts*

## THOSE RED ROCKS ARE QUITE THE COMMON SIGHT AROUND TOWN

Three-foot-by-two-foot-by-one-foot rectangular sandstone steps mark the entrance of my father's house. The massive blocks of stone came from a Manchester quarry, which was once located near the mall. Like they do at many of the local homes built in the early to late 1800s, the native rocks provide an entranceway if not a foundation.

Today, the beautiful red coloring speaks of a time when Manchester was once a large central Connecticut lake, then a swamp with slow, meandering rivers and streams. Centuries ago, Manchester was the deposit site of sand filled with iron oxide. This iron became the glue that gelled the sand into hard rock. It was also the source of the red color as it oxidized.

The town has also used these rectangular slabs as markers, outlining parking spaces at various parks and alongside roads. You can still see the natural treasure of the community attached to the earth as you drive onto I-84 from the Cheney Tech entrance and venture up Buckland Road.

Sandstone is a sedimentary rock, made up mostly of sand that was deposited in the bottom of a lake, which, under time's pressure, formed into rock. The sand is usually bound together by silica, calcium carbonate or iron oxide. Sandstone is relatively soft and easy to work with, which makes it a common building material.

Most visitors cross the Moon Bridge located in Wickham Park's Chinese Garden section. *Author's photograph.*

The quarrying of sand stone started early in Manchester's history. Charles Wolcott opened a quarry in the Buckland area. From this dig, dinosaur bones came to light. His quarry was then purchased in the late 1800s by the Gorman brothers (Michael and Patrick). This quarry provided the town with the crimson building blocks for nearly a century.

Cutting out these large slabs involved tremendous manual labor, as quarrymen had to first hand drill a series of one-inch- to two-inch-long holes along a natural seam or band in the rock. Workers then filled these holes with wedges and shims (feathers). These last two items were then hand driven by hammer into the stone until the rock split. The natural layer lines and even the drill lines are still present on the stone steps at my father's house and on the stone at other homes.

Manchester sandstone was also made into gravestones. Many examples dot the various Manchester cemeteries.

The Gormans came to Manchester after the flood of 1869. Many of Manchester's bridges that were washed away by the disaster were either rebuilt or enlarged by the brothers, who also operated a granite quarry in

Glastonbury. Many of the homes built in Manchester in the 1880s and 1890s used stone furnished by the Gorman brothers. Over the years, the brothers expanded their business to include heavy trucking, masonry contracting and residential and commercial construction. This construction business employed many of the future general builders who made Manchester their home, including a young F. William Kanehl.

## HIGHLAND PARK AND CASE MOUNTAIN ARE GIFTS THAT KEEP GIVING

"Hartford is so small," my granddaughter said as she looked out from Lookout Mountain toward the unobstructed view of the capital. Besides the tall buildings that appeared to the three-year-old as small, she could also clearly see the south end of Main Street with the old high school building and the South Methodist Church.

Located along Spring Street, Highland Park Springs and the walkway to Lookout Mountain—also called Case Mountain—was the gift of the Case brothers and the paper industry. The brothers, Frederick, A. Wells and A. Willard, started manufacturing paper and cardboard products in the 1860s. The mill operated until 1972. To provide power for their mill, the brothers had a dam constructed across the Birch Mountain Brook, creating the pond that is now part of the park. Birch Mountain Brook becomes the Hop Brook after it joins with the Porter Brook.

The Case brothers' operations survived two disastrous fires: one in 1875 and another in 1915. Each time, the company rebuilt and remained in Manchester. The brothers' love of the community can still easily be seen. In 1903, A. Wells Case began constructing what is now called Highland Park as a resting place for his family and the workers of his company. (The stone bridge that dominates the park's landscaping was one of the first jobs my stonemason grandfather worked on when he immigrated to Manchester.) The completion of the park fell to A. Wells's son Lawrence. It was opened to the general public by the 1920s. Town historian Mathias Spiess understood the value of the park when he wrote in 1923, "By preserving the natural beauty of this tract and making it accessible to the townspeople, the Cases have performed a notable public service."

Besides the nature walk and beautiful landscaping, Highland Park hides other natural features. At various times, the area hosted a copper mine

The Highland Park Bridge is one of the first projects the author's grandfather worked on as an immigrant to Manchester. *Author's photograph.*

operation. The ore rests in the stone foundation of the Highland Park area. Historian William Buckley explained in his history of Manchester, "In very early colonial times; efforts were made at different periods to mine it profitably. All failed because of the low quality of the ore." Other mining companies reopened shafts in the mid-1800s and kept them open into the early 1900s. As with the original miners, their efforts proved unprofitable. In 1973, Buckley wrote, "The opening of a shaft bored into the side of the cliff-like hill in the woods north of Spring Street can still be found." He also noted that one of Connecticut's most scenic waterfalls flows near the park. "Wyllys Falls is not the waterfall of the dam and the rapids below the stone bridge at Case's Pond." This natural wonder cuts its way over a Birch Mountain cliff in the woods just southwest of the park.

Highland Park does have one more gift: Highland Spring. This spring of mineral water was once nationally renowned for its power to cure. It was originally bottled by the Case brothers and then by other companies. Bottles of "Highland Rock Water" and "Highland Tonic Water" were sold throughout the nation as a natural curing tonic. Like the mineral water that brought people to the spa in Stafford Springs, Manchester's water was advertised as being a viable part of a water cure-all remedy for all kinds of ailments. Until the mid-1970s, it was common to find Manchester families making the weekly trip to the spring outlet near the stone bridge to fill plastic jugs.

# WICKHAM PARK

Racing down the steep hill that borders Manchester and East Hartford on a toboggan or sled is a thrill enjoyed by youngsters and adults in the area. This hill draws walkers and strollers in the summer months, as well as young children tumbling over and over as gravity pulls them toward the town line.

Wickham Park attracts people young and old not just for the adventures on the massive hill, which at one time provided passersby with an excellent view of Clarence Horace Wickham's home known as "the Pines," but for the whole outside experience. The 140-acre site came to the town in 1960 through the will of Edith Wickham. A few years later, an additional 63 acres of land were donation by neighbor Myrtle Williams. To this day, Wickham Park features a bird aviary that includes peacocks and other injured birds receiving care. It also contains a 1920s Italian shrine, an Oriental garden, an Irish garden and other various themed pavilions scattered around the more-than-two-hundred-acre park for simple sitting the reflecting.

Yearly, the site is filled with cars from around the state to watch the best cross-country runners from middle and high school compete in championship races. My son represented Oliver Wolcott Technical High School there over ten years ago. I covered other runners for the newspaper as they raced over the hills and valleys of the course forty years ago.

In the winter, the children in my family met a red-clad visitor who promised them, if they were good, presents would appear under a pine tree located in their living room.

Horace J. Wickham, Clarence Horace Wickham's father, invented the machine that produces stamped envelopes and wrappers for postage. This 1870s invention helped create the Plimpton Manufacturing Company of Hartford. Horace eventually had over twenty patents on such machines, which mass-produced envelopes and made it profitable for companies to manufacture them. Before his technology, letters were often just folded sheets of paper closed with a wax seal.

Clarence followed his father into the business and is credited with inventing window envelops, along with over twenty other patented modifications and perfections to envelope and wrapper production. He was also the supervisor in charge of manufacturing stamped envelopes and wrappers for the U.S. government. In Manchester, he organized the Hartford, Manchester, Rockville Tramway Company in the late 1880s. This trolley system developed Laurel Park, an end-of-the-line park that required a trolley ride to enter. The park sat across the highway from the current Wickham Park.

One of the oldest attractions at Wickham Park is this Italian shrine. *Author's photograph.*

Wickham Park was established under a trust fund when the Wickham estate was turned over to Manchester and East Hartford. The funds from the estate covered the cost to administrate the preparation and opening of the park. The park's trustees removed the family home from the property and set up play and picnic areas. The trustees still oversee the park and continually improve the site with new features.

Among the original venues that were created by the Wickhams is the park's Oriental garden, which has a tea house, a replica of a torii (a sacred Shinto shrine gateway) and a moon-bridge based on the Wickhams' many trips to China. While Clarence was in college, he met several Chinese students who were attending the school at the request of their government. Later, these friends held significant positions in the Chinese government. Items the Wickhams brought back from their trips fill the Oriental garden's reflection pathway.

Another Wickham feature is a log cabin that was rebuilt after a 1989 fire; it was meant to match a 1927 structure that the Wickhams used for "rustic" entertaining. Today, this cabin is the "North Pole" that children visit to meet Santa. It is also from this cabin that summer visitors can enjoy a vista, which allows them unobstructed views into Vernon, Hartford and beyond.

Aside from this park, the Wickhams financed the Wickham Memorial Library in East Hartford in honor of Clarence's parents. Edith Wickham also donated funds to support McGraft Park, which was named for her family, in her hometown of Muskegon, Michigan.

## HISTORY OF CENTER SPRINGS PARK PREDATES THAT OF OFFICIAL MANCHESTER

My granddaughter asked if Center Springs Park was a gift from the Cheney family, just like Center Memorial Park. It was, but nature and its location were more critical in its preservation.

After receiving the deed in the early 1900s, Manchester preserved this tree-and-grass-lined gully. This action helped establish Manchester's nickname, the City of Village Charm. The ravine marks the flow of Bigelow Brook and has been undeveloped throughout the town's centuries of settlements. Still, its importance as a central gathering place goes back even further in time—before there even was a Manchester.

The area itself has a long history as the site of a Native American settlement. The original residents of the Manchester area, the Podunk tribe, used the Center Springs area as a seasonal camping site. The locals found lamprey eels living in the springs and waterfalls, weaving their watery ways throughout the region. Ample lamprey and shad fish provided nourishment, and shade from the abundant trees provided a serene environment during the hot Connecticut summers. According to town historians, the Podunk tribe had several campsites all around the Manchester area. They traveled to these sites throughout the year. The one located at what is now Center Springs was their adopted home during the early spring. While at the springs, the Natives harvested lamprey and shad.

At one point, the brook flowed not only along the ravine to a small pond, but also parallel to East Center Street in the area that houses the high school today. This brook was powerful enough to entice the fish and eel, and it also took the life of a well-respected minister at Center Congregational Church. Elisha Cook, while crossing Bigelow Brook one day, fell from a downed tree bridge, struck his head and drowned in the water.

As the center of the town developed, the residents reengineered and rechanneled the brook, helping to create a recreational park to be enjoyed by residents in the tree-filled valley. The local millworkers of the 1800s enjoyed fishing and taking refreshing walks. The small pond created a natural ice-skating rink for the winter months, and the town built a log cabin to be used as a warming location for the skaters. Many residents remember shooting down the ravine's slope on either a sled or, more commonly, a toboggan.

Several visitors to the museum noted that this pond was the location of their first ventures on ice skates—both figure skates and long, thicker hockey skates. As leisure time increased and family-centered activities became the focus of residents, the skating lodge also became a place to meet Santa Claus during the Christmas holiday season. Other visitors added that in the mid-1960 and 1970s, they often walked through the site on their way to the Parkade Shopping Center and met friends there in the summer months.

The Parks and Recreation Department housed its offices in the building, which sits alongside the pond today. This building has offered preschool playgroups, classes and other activities.

As the town's residents' taste has matured, biking trails and walking trails have been constructed and maintained in the park. Now, age is appearing in some of the facilities. The residents have stepped up to the plate and voted to fund a restoration of the park for future residents.

## *Afterword*

My wife noted that, as a young girl, she saw her first streaker in the park. The park's natural cover of trees and brushes provided an excellent venue for the naked running fad of the mid-1970s.

## Union Pond Making Comeback from Polluted Past in Service to the Mills

"If you catch it, you can keep it," my wife called out to our youngest granddaughter, knowing full well that it will never happen. The geese waddle up toward my granddaughters, begging for food and then racing away the moment the girls try to catch them.

My granddaughters marvel at the abundant wildlife at Union Pond, making us wonder how this jewel within Manchester came to be. A dam on the Hockanum River, which was initially constructed for the water-powered mills of the 1800s, created the pond. The pond has undergone a significant

Surrounded by mill complexes, Union Pond once provided power, but today, it provides a respect to life's endeavors. *Author's photograph.*

revitalization since I was a child. The changes are dramatic when compared to the lake my father swam in and boated on.

Union Pond was initially the millpond for the Union Cotton Mill and the Oakland Paper Company. The first mill was one of the oldest and most successful cotton mills in the state, and the latter mill was one of the oldest paper mills in the state of Connecticut. The Oakland Mill produced the paper for the *Hartford Current*, initially called the *Connecticut Current*. That newspaper is the oldest continuously published paper in the United States. The paper mill sat above the pond, and the cotton mill spooled textiles below the dam. Both industries thrived in the mid- to late 1800s. They employed many of the residents in the North End of the town.

Unionville, as the area around the mills came to be known, was a significant municipality section of the town, rivaling and surpassing, at times, the Green and South Manchester in population and commercial development. It was this area that the Hartford, Providence and Fishkill Railroad brought tracks to that connected Manchester with Hartford, Willimantic and the rest of the world. Neither South Manchester nor the Green were considered enough of commercial hubs for the railroad companies to extend tracks to them. The Cheney brothers did build a private railroad from the south to connect to the Manchester station. Depot Square became the hub of the Unionville section and included the Old Union School. This name was dropped in the 1920s when the town constructed the Robertson School.

Besides the Union and Oakland Mills, other companies gathered in the area. Several of the mill complexes are still in use today—not for manufacturing, however. The large brick factory built by the Mather Electric

Company is one such building. It served as the home of the Bon Ami Soap Company and is now the Time Machine Hobby Store.

Union Pond fell into disarray as the Union Mills closed, and then, it disappeared. Older residents of the North End have recalled that the water would turn different colors based on what soap the Bon Ami Company was producing that day. Most residents tended not to swim there as my father had done. He contracted rheumatic fever there when he was young and silly enough to swim there.

By the time I began visiting the pond, it was clean enough for boating. As a Boy Scout, I learned to canoe on the waterway. Our scoutmaster selected the pond because it had a robust active current, which made us steer the canoe aggressively to hit a designated spot across the pond.

## DANCING BEARS HAVE BEEN GREETING RESIDENTS FOR OVER A CENTURY

"Let's go see the dancing bears," my granddaughters always say as we go to Center Park. Instantly, flashes of memories pass through my brain as I recall my sons all wanting to climb up the pedestal to see the bears. I remember making the same request myself as a child.

Longtime members of the Manchester family, the two bronze cubs in Center Park have been greeting visitors for more than a century. They have witnessed some of the most remarkable events in the history of Manchester—from road races and fires to town celebrations. The fountain is famous not just in town, but throughout the state. It is the centerpiece of a Cheney family gift, which tends to be overlooked by their other achievements and generosity. These gifts made Manchester a town for all, not just a reflection of a wealthy manufacturing family.

The *Dancing Bears* came from the artistic mind of Charles Adams Platt. He was the son of Mary Elizabeth Cheney, a daughter of mill founder George Welles Cheney. Platt designed the fountain to honor his uncle Frank Cheney, who was also a founding brother of the mills. The fountain joined the park in 1909, a few years after Frank Cheney's death. Platt was considered one of the family's best artists, which is impressive considering there were two internationally renowned artists among his uncles (Seth and John). A third internationally famous artist (Russell) was his cousin.

The other Charles Platt fountain found in Manchester. This one honors Revolutionary War soldiers. *Author's photograph.*

The actual sculptor of the fountain was Albert Humphreys of New York. He sculpted the bears on a commission from the Cheney family. Humphreys had studied painting in Paris along with Platt at the Académie Julian.

Platt later put aside his art to follow an architectural career. He specialized in designing large homes with gardens for the wealthy families of the late 1800s. You can see an example of his work in what was once the home of Frank Cheney Jr.; it is located on the corner of Hartford Road and Main Street. This building is now the office of the chamber of commerce and still maintains many of the features Platt was famous for incorporating in his designs. Three other homes along Hartford Road were designed by Platt, as were the homes of the Rockville Maxwell brothers. One of these homes now houses the hospital. Another example of Platt's work is the Elks Lodge on North Park Street. Platt based his career in New York City, where he designed museums, commercial buildings and homes. However, his *Dancing Bears* fountain remains his most-beloved piece of art by the younger residents of Manchester.

You can find another fountain that Platt designed for Manchester in the park. It is located next to the probate court and honors the veterans of the American Revolution. This fountain was originally the center divider of Main and Center Streets. Before the roundabout was at the top of the hill, the fountain was the middle of the four-way intersection. It was hit too many times by cars and had to be removed. The fountain was returned to the center of town in the late 1980s. For many years, it stood at the sanitation office near the town dump.

# Center Park: A Gathering Place for Manchester

"Let's race to the flag" is the common request when I take my granddaughters to the Mary Cheney Library. After a little while of looking at books and DVDs, they want to get out and enjoy the lovely park located around the building. However, this run was almost made impossible. In both 1977 and 2003, the town was interested in paving much of the seven acres of sprawling lawn for parking. Concerned citizens stopped the proposals, allowing my grandchildren the chance to race to the flag.

When summer arrives, like most Manchester residents, my family gathers at Center Park. Most of us, at some time this season, will assemble to participate in arts and crafts, concerts and other downtown events. The park that is officially called the Center Memorial Park was a gift from the Cheney family. Susan Cheney, the wife of Frank Cheney, one of the founding brothers of the silk mills, presented the land that now surrounds the library to the town. In 1905, she received permission to establish and design the park, and eventually, it became town property in 1912. It is fascinating to note that Susan was also the mother of Mary Cheney. Her name graced the new library building when it was constructed in 1937, long after Susan had passed away.

The land that Susan landscaped in1905 abutted other property at the center of town that had previously been given or sold to Manchester by the Cheney family. These parcels of land were presented to hold the original hall of records, now the probate court, that was built in 1896. Another slice of land was given to the town for the erection of the Civil War memorial in 1877. Susan Cheney also presented the *Dancing Bears* fountain, which is another frequent stop for my granddaughters, to the town. This fountain was dedicated to the memory of her husband and was erected in 1909, a few years after his death.

The Cheney family's handprints are visible everywhere in Center Memorial Park. Besides donating the actual land, the Cheney family was instrumental in designing several of the items located there. As mentioned before, the *Dancing Bears* fountain that memorializes Frank Cheney was designed by his nephew Charles Adams Platt. Another family member, Frank C. Farley, designed the Mary Cheney Library. Nationally famous Platt also designed the flagpole memorial and the slowly raising steps that ascend the long sweeping knoll that dominates half of the property. Today's version of the site honors Mary Olmstead Chapman, a longtime member of the town's park commission.

Situated at the top of the ridge, which divides Main Street from the south to the north, the park has served as a gathering place. Here, residents have gathered for Memorial Day speeches, political rallies, art and craft shows and evening concerts in honor of pride in Manchester. What I remember the most, as a child, however, is the gathering of snow sled riders. Sledding down the sloop, from the flagpole toward the library, has thrilled innumerable children. Only the erection of the manger scene during the Christmas season spoiled this ride. Today, the manger scene is erected on the lawn of the First Congregational Church, keeping the snow run at the Center Park open at all times, inviting to the youths of Manchester.

# The Woodbridge Barn and Agricultural Roots

I took my granddaughters to the Manchester Historical Society's restoration of Woodbridge Barn at the Green. On the way home, my oldest granddaughter pointed out several other barns that are still visible to a child riding in the back seat. This enthusiastic pointing out of barns caused me to reflect on the barns of Manchester in general.

Initially, the town was a farming community. Its agricultural past is often overlooked. The study of the mills and industries that came to settle in Manchester tends to get more attention.

The Woodbridge property, located on the western end of the Manchester Green, was a working dairy farm until 1949. Still, the farm's barns remained long after their economic livelihood had ended. The Manchester Historical Society believes the restored barn dates from at least 1774.

Driving around Manchester, you can still see various examples of the town's agricultural history. Just up East Center Street from the Green, there's a large red barn from the 1800s. This property contains the remains of the Cone and Wadsworth Carriage Firm. The old carriage shop, a blacksmith shop and the barn all remain today to speak of the early Manchester industry. Other barns near the Green include the impressive gray barn, nested on its

The Woodbridge Barn dates back to before the founding of the United States. *Author's photograph.*

stone foundation, of the old Wickham property. This site was the home of Horace Wickham, the inventor; he also helped bring the trolleys to town. His son was the one who gave us Wickham Park.

Along the fringes of town, you can locate other agriculturally oriented barns. Some still operate as farm outbuildings; others show their age and are collapsing in on themselves. These dinosaurs speak of a time when families may have worked in factories but also maintained a cow, a horse and some pigs for food.

As you venture near the East Hartford and South Windsor Line, you can retrace when Connecticut was a significant producer of shade tobacco. Several examples of the multi-louvered sided tobacco barns can be found. I'm sure many of you remember working tobacco in the summers. My parents met each other because of the local crop. My mother was one the "Georgia Girls" who was brought north to work the fields. Hollywood captured this bit of Connecticut history in its movie *Parrish*. If you look closely at the drama, you'll see my mother, one of the many extras they hired while filming in the area.

The barns and carriage houses that genuinely fascinate me are the large buildings in the middle of the residential and business zones of Manchester that are still actively used today. These former livestock homes shelter the family auto and business supplies stores. Many are located just off our main streets. These structures have been modified from their original designs, but still, they sing of their original purpose.

The Woodbridge Barn clearly shows the New England habit of reusing and recycling materials. Manchester residents have reassigned their various farm barns to new occupations, providing added years to these structures' lives and providing us with living fossils of the past. Take a moment to ride around town and find these fossils. You may be surprised by the number of them.

## THE GAME OF GOLF HAS A STORIED AND EGALITARIAN HISTORY IN TOWN

Chasing the Whiffle golf ball around the backyard with the plastic clubs is an activity enjoyed by not only my granddaughters but also by their father when he was young and numerous other Manchester children. For some, this simple activity grows into the mania known as golf.

Longtime town and state official Nate Agostinelli recently recalled some of the most interesting stories of his life. One of these stories included the accomplishment that was Manchester's ability to purchase the land of the Manchester Country Club. Residents gained not only a golf course but also a reservoir and about one thousand acres that came with the sale. This purchase, he felt, was incredibly lucky for the town and its residents. "Many people do not realize how much land is there and how wonderful it is that it has remained undeveloped," he said. The current Manchester Country Club's land is owned by the town, as Agostinelli noted, and it was purchased by a vote of the people. Because it is a public and private course, golf has become a game in Manchester that is not just for the rich.

Golf has been a mania in Manchester for well over one hundred years, starting long before the current facility opened on South Main Street in 1917. South Manchester and the Cheney family had a long history of love for the game. They were not just involved with the creation of the Manchester Country Club, but they were also involved with the creation of a golf team that dominated the state championships in the early 1900s. It was an all-Cheney team, by the way. Operating out of the Orford Golf Club, this team produced some of the best golfers in the state.

The Orford Club Course was located where the current high school sits. This course had nine holes and served to help establish the popularity of golf in Manchester. Besides being the local golf course, the site also served as the site for the community's fireworks and other celebrations. A newspaper article from 1897 noted that a local builder constructed the Orford Clubhouse in two days; the house was twenty feet by thirty feet and divided into two rooms, a locker and a club room.

The Orford Club was an organization that the Cheneys oversaw and maintained. Besides local golf activities, the building hosted town receptions. The land just south of the course, where a tennis court currently stands, was the home of Timothy Cheney, one of the oldest houses in town. It's dismantling in the 1960s caused the creation of the Manchester Historical Society.

Interestingly, Orford also allowed women to join, according to a *Connecticut Magazine* article from 1900 that was preserved at the Manchester Historical Society. This magazine on state golf courses noted, "There are a number of young women in the club who are good players, and some of the ladies are officers of the organization being represented on the committees."

The Cheney family set aside the land by the Globe Hollow Reservoir for the construction of a new nine-hole golf course in the early 1900s.

The Orford Golf Clubhouse overlooked the original golf course in town. *Postcard from the author's collection.*

After playing on it for a few years, the family brought in Tom Bendelow and Deveroux Emmet. They were top golfers of the time. They set out an eighteen-hole course, which has remained basically the same since 1917.

Besides the current links on South Main Street, there were other courses in Manchester. Just off Slater Road, the road many people use today to get to the mall, there was a nine-hole course called "Red Rock." This course was in operation until the early 1980s. The expansion of the highway and the development of the Buckland Hills area caused the owners to close and sell. Unfortunately for residents, Fox Grove's Golf Course on Keeney Street also closed around the same time. This 270-plus-acre site was sold to house developers, and by 1973, the land had become housing lots.

Closures and redesign also struck in the 1980s, as the Minnechaug Golf Course just over the Manchester line in Glastonbury was remodeled from eighteen holes to nine holes. The remaining land was also sold off for housing. Located just south from the Manchester Country Club, this Glastonbury course had provided young observers in the 1960s and 1970s an almost endless green lawn along South Main.

## *Afterword*

This column was selected by the Manchester historian to be retained on the society's web page as a permanent link. The town referendum of 1955 was included as the purchase date, as was the fact that Globe Hollow Reservoir was part of the one-dollar sell-off of Cheney property in the 1930s.

# 9

# *Interesting People*

## CEMETERY VISIT REVEALS THE GRIM LIVES OF MANY FORMER RESIDENTS

Walking through any old cemetery, you cannot help but notice how hard life must have been for the people in the 1700s and up to the 1900s. A grouping of Pitkin family grave markers in the Buckland Cemetery clearly shows this.

Several white marble markers from the end of the 1800s to the early 1900s bear the Pitkin name. Of these, only one person identified lived what we would consider a long life; Emily R., as she is remembered, lived to the age of eighty-seven. The other Pitkins in this small collection of graves only reached middle or early adulthood. Two were in their fifties at the time of their deaths; one died in 1916 and the other in 1918. The second may have been a victim of the influenza pandemic, which struck the nation after the First World War. In this group, two other Pitkins died before mid-life; Ella A. died at the age of thirty-one in 1879, and William C. died at the age of forty-four in 1863. And Charles M. Pitkin died at the age of twenty in 1878.

Not far from this group of markers is a large stone for Doctor William Cooley. William Cooley's name appeared in the town's history as being one of the town officials who was elected at Manchester's first town meeting. He was named a hayward, which was an official who was put in charge of

*Above*: Located in a Manchester cemetery, this grave marker tells the plight of many young ladies. *Author's photograph.*

*Left*: This marker for Mary Gilman shows the respect early residents placed on motherhood. *Author's photograph.*

hedges and fences to make sure cattle did not ruin crops. He was the same William Cooley who fought in the War of 1812 and escaped from a British prisoner of war camp. His father was Dr. Samuel Cooley of Bolton. He housed the famous artist Ralph Earl and the inventor and marketer of a well-known 1800s digestive medicine called Cooley's Bitters.

William's grave notes that he lived to be fifty-eight years old before dying in 1839. Right under his name are the names of three women: Mary Buckland, who died at age twenty-two in 1812; Diantha Spencer, who also died at twenty-two in 1817; and Jerusha Pitkin, who lived to be eighty-nine before dying in 1891. Were these the three wives of the dear doctor? (Women often died young from overwork, illness or childbirth.)

Whether you travel through the Buckland Cemetery, East Cemetery or West Cemetery, you will find the grave makers of little children. It was not uncommon in colonial days to almost modern times for children to die before their fifth birthdays. Markers in the town cemeteries bear this out.

Another sad fact is that, after the Civil War, many Connecticut families migrated out west, spurred on by the stories that were brought back by the soldiers of the West's fertile farmland. With these facts in mind, I stumbled on a small grave for Charles G., the son of Cyrus and Mary Goodale. Young Charles died January 14, 1837, at the age of eight months. His grave is even more sad, for as are no other Goodales nearby. What happened to his father, Cyrus, or his mother, Mary?

My favorite maker in Buckland Cemetery is Mary Gilman's stone. The inscription speaks not only of the strength of the colonial woman who is remembered, but also of the different language we have developed over time. The letter *f*, at the time, was commonly used to represent the letter *s*. The stone boldly reads:

> *In Memory of Mrs. Mary confort* [consort] *of Enf* [Ens.] *Solomon Gilman—who died Auguft* [August] *28ᵗʰ 1786 in 68ᵗʰ year of her age. She was Mother of 12 children left 11 of them living.*

Mary's husband was one of the petitioners who gained Orford Parish's independence. One of her eleven surviving children, Solomon Jr., fought in the Revolutionary War.

## THE MILKMAN WAS A FREQUENT VISITOR BACK IN THE DAY

There was once a man who knew your routine better than your best friend. He arrived before the sun with the intelligence of what morning beverage you preferred and how much you needed between visits. He knew if there was a new child or even if visitors were staying for a while in your house. He was the milkman.

My granddaughters were amazed to learn that there was a time when milk did not come in plastic jugs at the store but was delivered right there at the doorstep.

Many times, when I was young, I would open a silver box with a lid that prevented snow and rain from getting in to find a bottle of fresh milk. We also placed the empty bottles in the box, and the delivery man exchanged these empties weekly with filled bottles from his carrier.

Manchester, like many towns across the country, had several local dairies and milk dealers that provided the delivery of milk to the town's houses. I remember growing up on Porter Street and seeing the Dart's Dairy across the street from me. The Dart Building on East Center Street continues the dairy's memory with its name. Other dairies were found almost throughout the entire town, not just in what we would consider the farming outskirts of town. The addresses found in old town directories are surprising.

The Woodbridge family maintained a dairy on the farm at the Green. It operated until the late 1940s, when the state required that all dairies begin pasteurizing their milk. Shady Glen, the restaurant, was also a dairy. Bottles from that dairy still decorate Manchester houses, as well as shelves in area antique stores.

Among the various antique collections, I have found the following Manchester milk bottles: Dart's Dairy (East Center Street), West Side (Joseph Trueman and Sons, McKee Street), Wilkie (Arthur R. Wilkie, Walker Street), Shady Glen (John Rieg, Middle Turnpike East), Woodside Farms (B.R. Keeney, Keeney Street) and Oak Grove Dairy (H. Sankey, Oakland Street).

The Manchester Directory of 1939 lists eighteen milk dealers. The names included the following (not including those noted above): John Boyle's farm on East Middle Turnpike; Bryant and Chapman on Holl Street; Case Brothers on Birch Mountain Road; Center Spring Dairy on Edgerton Street; Thomas Graham on Edgerton Street; Clifford Keeney on Keeney Street; Edward Lynch on Vernon Street; Raymond Miller on Spencer Street; Hulda Nielson on Parker Street; Straughan's Diary on

East Center Street; Sunshine Dairy on Academy Street; Waranoke Dairy on Porter Street; and North Elm Dairy on North Elm Street.

In 1952, there were just six dairies listed; one was located in East Hartford. By 1974, the directory only listed two remaining dairies: Dart Mart on Main Street and Dari Maid Milk Co. of Keeney Street.

My grandmother had milk delivered almost until her death in the 1970s. There was nothing like having to skim the cream from the top of the bottle for cooking. That's what made her rice pudding so good.

As a reporter in the late 1980s, I wrote about the area farms here and in Glastonbury. The one story that I could not get was Mr. Keeney's retirement after fifty years as a milkman. He refused to be interviewed, thinking there would not be much of a story. Just imagine what memories he had of the town and of the people he served during cold winter nights and family celebrations.

Recently, I have seen advertisements on the internet for milk delivery once again. What is the saying? "What is old becomes new once again."

## Town Has an Impressive History of High-Ranking Military Leaders

My granddaughters noted one day that my history books all seemed to be about wars. War dominates history—fortunately or unfortunately. As historians and history buffs, we find ourselves looking to the leaders in those times to inspire us in the times we face today. One historian noted that people study these historical figures to see if they, in times of trouble, could be just as strong a leader themselves. I will not address that issue. I will only ask you to think about it.

Manchester has experienced several major wars throughout the history of the United States and a few "police actions." Among the residents of Manchester, our participation in these events has been significant and sacrificial. Shakespeare wrote in *Henry V*, "If we are marked to die, we are enough. To do our country loss; and if to live, the fewer men, the greater share of honor." The same can be said of the Manchester residents who gave their last full measures for the nation. They are enough to give us all grief. Among the lucky ones who came home, there was greater glory.

The question remains, however: Who were the leaders? Manchester has produced five men who reached brigadier general rank: John L. Otis, Sherwood Cheney, Daniel Bissell, James McVeigh and Nate Agostinelli.

After the Revolutionary War, Manchester resident Daniel Bissell opted to remain in the new nation's army. This devotion was reflective of his father (Ozias), a Revolutionary army officer who was buried in East Cemetery, and his brother Russell. The latter died as a major in the United States Army. Daniel served in the frontier of the nation. He was appointed the military governor of Upper Louisiana by President Thomas Jefferson before retiring and settling in St. Louis, Missouri, where he died in 1833. His promotion to brigadier general came in 1814, during the War of 1812.

The Civil War produced Brevet Brigadier General John L. Otis. Otis was a local manufacturer who had connections to the mills at the Green and along Hop Brook. He enlisted as a second lieutenant in the Tenth Connecticut Volunteer Infantry and saw actions in over fourteen engagements. His bravery quickly earned him promotions, and he became the colonel of the regiment by 1863. His superiors highly praised his efforts at Petersburg. He was wounded twice during the war and was given the honor of writing the official history of the One Hundredth Connecticut. After the war, he returned to Manchester for a short time. He then moved to Massachusetts, where his manufacturing company prospered. He continued to be involved in several veteran organizations in Connecticut as well as Massachusetts.

Sherwood Cheney, a subject of his own column, served the nation from the Spanish-American War to just before the Second World War, reaching the rank of brigadier general at the end of the First World War.

James H. McVeigh, also from Manchester, also reached brigadier general status and, like Cheney, was noted as an organizer and trainer. McVeigh served in the First World War and with the national guard between wars. During the Second World War, he was assigned to the office of inspector general, first in Washington, D.C., then in London, where he oversaw the training and efficiency of the American troops in Europe. McVeigh played an active role in the Normandy Invasion and continued in active duty after the war. He retired as a brigadier general in 1952 and returned to Manchester.

Nate Agostinelli served as an enlisted man during the Korean conflict. His career as an officer came with his service in the Connecticut Army National Guard, where he reached the rank of brigadier general. He was appointed by the secretary of the army to be his civilian aide, representing Connecticut, and he was the director of selective service for the state under President Clinton. In town, Agostinelli also handled various state and town offices during his lifetime.

## *Afterword*

My granddaughter once asked which I liked better, writing for a newspaper or writing books. I noted that writing books involved a lot of alone time, while writing for a newspaper involved a lot of talking to people. What is good about newspaper writing is that people instantly share their ideas and thoughts with you, especially if you miss something on a topic. This sharing comes quickly enough that corrections and additional facts appear in the media while the memory of the newspaper article is still relevant. Dialogue and responses about a book, however, generally happen well after the writer—and even the reader—has moved on to another project.

One of the reasons I became a history major in school was because I could not remember anyone of importance other than the Cheneys coming from Manchester. It was amazing to discover that five men from Manchester had reached the rank of general. Still, that number was quickly challenged when the column appeared.

This column on generals sparked an instant response from one missed general and a friend who knew of two modern holders of the rank. The three names I missed were David Gay, David Boland and Veto Addabbo. All three men served this nation not only in active duty, but also in the reserves and with national guard, which was where they all achieved their general ranks.

Garden roses are a common sight because of the efforts of Manchester's Burr family. *Author's photograph.*

Boland was a Manchester High School graduate and became a brigadier general in the army national guard after the Vietnam Conflict.

Addabbo also attended Manchester High School and was the son of a well-known tailor on Spruce Street. He earned his one-star general rank with the air national guard in the 2000s.

Finally, Gay was a resident of the town for many years before moving to Windsor. He became a major general with the Connecticut National Guard in 1992. His official residence, which was listed as Windsor, fooled this researcher, and I am sorry for that.

## TOWN RESIDENTS WERE BIG NAMES
### IN GARDENING AND LANDSCAPING

The warm sun has reached into the houses and hearts of gardeners across the town. Manchester residents have begun planting seeds, seedlings and even full-size bushes and plants as they have tried to find a constructive way to ride out the COVID-19 outbreak at home.

These always-optimistic tenders of the ground know how to bring color, fragrance and pure joy into the world for themselves, their neighbors and anyone who happens to pass by their homes. My wife gets excited any day someone passes by with a shout of, "Your gardens look great," or, "I love what you have done to your house." Gardening is in the blood of Manchester. Two vital people from Manchester have tickled the green thumbs of all would-be landscape artists.

Luther James Olcott, the grass master, came from the West End. He grew up on what is now Olcott Street. In the late 1800s, he spent his time studying grass and the different plants that could be crossed-bred and fertilized to bring about the perfect carpet of green. On a one-acre parcel of land near the old Olcott Homestead, James maintained a research field. This field held over 1,500 distinct specimens of grass from around the country and the world.

As a landscape artist, Frederick Law Olmsted used Olcott's advice on how to grow the best green carpet in designing New York's Central Park and Hartford's Bushnell Park. Olmsted was from Hartford himself and is considered to have been one of the first landscape artists in the nation. Olcott's work can also be seen in Brooklyn's Prospect Park, as well as in the private homes of the wealthy of the late 1800s—and even sports arenas today. Olcott's West Cemetery grave originally had a covering of different grasses that he had perfected. Over time, however, this unique covering has become overgrown with other native grasses that were too healthy to be held back—much like native Manchester residents.

Another gardening team was the father-and-son duo of Clifford and Charles Burr. They helped develop the idea of wholesaling bushes and landscaping plants across the state and the country. Senior Burr started his Burr Nursery in the North End, near the Apel Opera House. It eventually spread to the vast acreage of land known as Burr's Corner, which was located near today's mall. The company grew plants for shipment around the world.

Burr's company grew from door-to-door salesmen who visited farmers and house owners, offering the plants that would change the nation. Burr

Nursery was famous for its bushes and ornamental trees, as well as its native and landscaping plants.

The Burr family also sought the universal perfection of flowering plants, and they centered this goal on establishing heartiness, making it possible to ship live plants across the nation. The company also helped develop the machinery and the process that allowed for the shipment of live plants. Many of these processes are still in use today. Among the machines they perfected were a pneumatic rose-packing machine and a wrapping and tying machine.

Even more astonishing were the roses that came from this town. Charles Burr devoted his lifetime to the perfection of roses and the graphing of rose plants. His roses provided color and fragrance not only for the homes in the area, but for homes around the world. His devotion to this one plant made him a household name nationwide. The names of roses he developed are American Flagship, Merry Heart, Cherry Glow, First Lady, First Love, Angelique, Peace, Imperial Queen, Chrysler Imperial, Queen Elizabeth, Imperial Gold, Gold Glow and Gay Debutante.

Besides its Oakland Street and Burr Corner locations, the Burr Company maintained storage facilities on Hilliard Street. These refrigerated warehouses helped preserve the health of the various plants that stopped there on their way to permanent homes around the world.

## Art was More than Just a Hobby for the Cheney Family

Art runs in my granddaughter's blood as it did in the blood of Manchester's leading family. From painting to sculptures, art dominated the lives of several Cheney sons and daughters.

The founding brothers' generation produced two nationally renowned artists: Seth and John. Seth was a portrait artist who provided financial backing for the mill when money was tight. His portraits of famous Bostonians, in particular, can still be found in history books across the nation. John was an engraver who also painted. His skill was not as recognized as his brother, but he also provided the needed funding for the mills to grow.

A future generation provided the nation with Russell Cheney (the son of Knight Dexter Cheney), a well-respected landscape artist of the early 1900s. His paintings captured the impressionistic style that was popular at the time with loose brushstrokes, primary colors and light. The New Britain Museum

Russell Cheney's style made him one of the family's most famous artists. This painting is of a display at the society. *Courtesy of the Manchester Historical Society.*

of American Art and the Wadsworth Antheneum, among other museums, still have his pieces in their collections. But both the Cheney Homestead and the Old Manchester Museum offer several of the family's artworks for viewing without leaving Manchester. The museums contain examples from Russell, John and Seth, as well as Dorothy and others connected to the family.

Beyond the actual Cheney artists, other family members strived for the continuation of artistic mediums. Money was donated and set aside for the continual advancement of art in a number of the family's wills. The Mary Cheney Library had funds donated from the Frank Cheney family for the development of women artists. The New Britain Museum of American Art still brings the artistic experience to young generations through many programs and exhibits in the Cheney Gallery on the second floor of the museum. The Wadsworth displays not only art pieces created by Cheneys, but also several non-Cheney art works, silk and furniture that has been donated to the family's collection.

What is not as well known is the contribution that the architectural side of the family brought to the art world. Charles Adams Platt, the son of Mary Cheney and John Platt, was the designer of the bear fountain next

Russell Cheney also painted this version of his family's homestead, just one of four he did to capture the structure in all seasons. *Courtesy of the Manchester Historical Society.*

to the Mary Cheney Library. He also provided the American Impressionist movement a place to exhibit and sell its art.

In the early 1900s, a group of American artists gathered at Old Lyme to experiment and perfect their impressionist style, which was modeled after the French movement of Monet, Renoir and Degas. Among these artists staying at the Florence Griswold House were Metcalf and Hassam, who were destined to become leading American Impressionists. Their paintings captured the attention of the world, and soon, a colony of other artists joined the Griswold House. The only problem was that there was not a place to truly exhibit their work in Old Lyme. In 1914, Platt came to the colony and donated his time and skill, designing the first gallery for the newly formed Lyme Art Association. The First World War prevented the gallery's construction until 1920. This exhibit hall served as the launching point of many future artists.

Not just an architect, Platt also has pieces of artwork in the New Britain collection.

# EDNAH DOW CHENEY HAS A CONNECTION TO FAMOUS LITTLE WOMEN AUTHOR

One of the pictures nominated for an Academy Award this past season (at the time this article was published) was developed from the mind of Mary Louis Alcott. What may not be understood is that Manchester has a fascinating relationship with this writer.

Ednah Dow Cheney, the second wife of Seth Cheney, is not just a forgotten member of the family; she had a history of her own that rivaled the most famous people of her time. Her fame reaches into our century, as seen with films like *Little Women*. Ednah's biographies of her friend Mary Louis Alcott helped keep the writer's stories alive in the hearts of future generations.

Ednah Dow Littlehale was born in Boston and lived there for most of her life. In 1851, she helped found the Boston School of Design, one of the first co-ed schools for art. There, she met painter Seth Cheney, and she married him in 1853. At the time, Seth Cheney's talent had already captured the faces of many of Boston's rich and famous. Ednah and Seth traveled to Europe—as well as around New England—to study art in their first few years of marriage. Their daughter, Margaret, was also born during this time. The world of success seemed open to the young family, but then Seth's health started to fade. By 1856, he had died, leaving Ednah as a single parent. Ednah Cheney never remarried and returned to Boston to raise her daughter alone.

The Cheneys of Manchester did not forget her, though, and she was often a welcomed guest at the homes of the other Manchester brothers. In the town's history, a fuzzy picture from the late 1800s shows Ednah on the porch of Knight Dexter's house; it is accompanied by a caption that says that Aunt Ednah was a frequent household visitor.

Meanwhile, Ednah's life in Boston was centered on her daughter, Margaret, as well as education—especially education for women. Turning to philanthropy and reform, Ednah helped establish the New England Hospital for Women and Children. This institution provided medical training for women physicians. She also worked with women's clubs to foster other educational opportunities for women. Ednah was a frequent lecturer at various nationwide women's rights conventions and lobbied for equal rights as the vice president and later president of the New England Women's Suffrage Society.

Like many members of the suffrage movement, Ednah also helped the abolitionist cause. She supported freedom for the slaves before the Civil War, and then, she supported the education of the newly freed slaves after the war.

Her efforts with the New England Freedman's Aid Society helped established schools throughout the southern states as well as the freedman colleges.

Besides these focuses, Ednah became a member of the Transcendentalist movement, which was led by Bronson Alcott and Ralph Waldo Emerson. This group included the young Louisa May Alcott as well. In this group, Ednah became a friend of the writer. This friendship eventually developed the nucleus of Edna's two biographies: *Children's Friend* (1888), a sketch of Louisa May Alcott, and *Biography of L.M. Alcott* (1889). These works were the first biographies of the writer. They also contained quotes from the letters and diaries of the *Little Women* author that have disappeared with time. The books often are referenced by other studies done on Alcott.

Other books Ednah wrote include a biography of Seth and one of John Cheney, as well as a work about her daughter, Margaret. This young lady became one of the first women to enroll at Boston's Institute of Technology (now MIT), opening the school to women. While she was still a student, Margaret died of tuberculosis. A hint of her scientific talent does appear in an article she had published in a scientific journal that describes experiments with nickel, including a method of determining the presence of the metal in ore.

## Cheney Family Member Famous for More Than Spinning Silk

My grandchildren always point out the Cheney name on buildings and places. Growing up in Manchester, you cannot help but have heard the name Cheney. There is the Mary Cheney Library, Cheney Hall, Howell Cheney Technical School and, of course, the old Cheney mills. This list only names some of the more permanent structures associated with the name.

Like with all families, there is the opportunity—even among the patron family of Manchester—to be overlooked and overshadowed. Historians look at the seven Cheney brothers who started the silk industry and see two, John and Seth, who provided financial assistance while pursuing art careers. This example from the first generation shouts to us that not all the Cheneys went into the silk business—some even remained on the farm.

Buried in East Cemetery, in a small alcove of the Cheney family section, is the gravestone of one overlooked family member who was just as famous in his field as his silk-making family members were in their mills. A member of the third generation, Sherwood Cheney left the confines of Manchester

This painting of Colonel Sherwood Cheney looks down on visitors at the society's museum. *Courtesy of the Manchester Historical Society.*

to become a national figure. This son of John S. Cheney was born in South Manchester; he took the trolley and train into Hartford to attend Hartford Public High School since Manchester didn't have its own high school at the time. He earned enough recognition to be nominated to the U.S. Military Academy at West Point. After graduating from the cradle of the American Officer Corps, he served with the United States Army as a combat engineer. (Combat engineers are the people who build bridges while the enemy is firing at them. They are the people who locate and dig landmines out of the ground, sometimes while under hostile fire, but still, it's dangerous work even when no one is firing.) He saw active combat service in Cuba during the Spanish American War. More of his frontline service came in the Philippine Insurrection that followed. His cousin Lieutenant Ward Cheney died in action in the Philippines at this same time.

Sherwood's active duty continued at various posts in the United States. He rose to the rank of colonel before the beginning of the First World War. During that conflict, Sherwood Cheney traveled to France. His engineering, transportation and supply skills made him a chief standout for the American Expeditionary Forces. His efforts impressed the overall commander, General John J. Pershing, and his promotion to brigadier general came before the war was over.

General Pershing placed this native Manchester son in charge of bringing the troops home. His efforts in the quick, effortless process earned him the Distinguished Service Cross. Rumor has it that he was in charge of selecting the order in which soldiers went home (the Connecticut boys were not held waiting in France). Manchester claimed Sherwood as one of its own, and he responded in kind by bringing the Manchester troops back early in the rotation.

France also awarded Sherwood its Legion of Honor, the Croix de Guerre, for his actions during the war.

After the world war, the Manchester native remained in active duty. He served throughout the nation as a senior officer and represented the United States in China. He ended up becoming a military aide to President Calvin Coolidge. Not too bad for a boy from South Manchester.

After retiring from the service, he returned to Manchester, where he died in 1949.

One last thing he did was help found and support the Mystic Seaport Museum. This support continues to exemplify his effect on our world to this day—like that of his other family members.

## *Afterword*

This column created interest in an association related to Calvin Coolidge. This group asked me to write a chapter on Sherwood for its book on 1920s history. My research into Cheney surprised me with the discovery of the following achievements, which were not in the original column:

Cheney was actually a presidential aide for Teddy Roosevelt as well as Calvin Coolidge. He was involved in the final selection of the Panama Canal location. He was one of the first American soldiers to see the battlefield in France, as he conducted a needs assessment for the corps of engineers. His report's recommendations continue to be used in the modern corps. At the end of World War One, Cheney was involved in the negotiation of peace and the removal of German troops from the Baltic States. He served as commander of the army corps of engineers' training school. He saw action against Pancho Villa on the Mexican border. From 1918 to 1919, Cheney was the director general of transportation for the American forces in France. He oversaw the reworking of both the Boston and San Francisco Harbor regions in the 1920s and 1930s. He actually has a baseball card—a famous American Card that was produced by TOPPS. His grandfather was George Wells Cheney, the oldest of the seven mill founders. His father, John Sherwood Cheney, participated in the 1849 Californian gold rush as well as the Australian gold rush a few years later. While in Australia, John served as the mayor of Crestwick New South Wales. Like most of his brothers and cousins, Sherwood spent time working in the mills during his summer breaks, as the Cheney family expected the young men to learn the industry.

To repeat what I wrote in the original column—not too bad for a boy from South Manchester.

## This Cheney Was Known for Capturing the Town with His Artistic Talent

"Did you know a Cheney?" my granddaughter asked one day. "Not really," I answered, as most of the people of my generation can only envision the Cheney family members who were not involved with the mill operations. That complex was sold before my memory began. I knew of the Cheney who married Dr. Spock, the famous pediatrician. I once had a distant Cheney relative as a student in one of my classes. Pictures of matriarchal older ladies named Margreta and Emily, who wrote books about the Cheneys, also came to mind. But really, the only Cheney I could recall was the man who wore a dark suit coat and tan rumpled pants as he traveled around Manchester, his eyes scanning the whole town as if it was his backyard. Maybe it was. "No," I looked at my granddaughter. "I didn't know a Cheney, but your grandmother did."

My wife worked at the Corner Soda Shop on Main Street, near the old State Theater, now the Prayer Tower. Every day, she would serve Jake Cheney a donut on a pristine white paper plate, and he would leave her a memory. Jake often traveled around the center of town, his artistic eyes always looking for an image he could capture. In Manchester, his art was loved more than the works of his nationally famous relatives.

One visitor to the Old Manchester Museum noted that she was scared of the man who sat in the library one day, staring at her. Then, he presented her with a drawing of herself before he shuffled out of the door. "I wish I had saved it," she regretted. Another patron told me that his wife, while attending a meeting one night after they had first moved to town, became concerned with the elderly, well-dressed man who sat in the back of the room, studying her. "Oh, that was just Jake Cheney," she was told. "There's no harm there, just an artistic stare."

*Left*: Jake Cheney often handed people small portraits of themselves. This portrait was given to the waitress at the Corner Soda Shop. *Author's collection.*

*Right*: Jake Cheney also sketched daily objects if someone asked him to. *Author's collection.*

My wife talked with him daily. She made friendly conversation with the older man, talking of her adventures and needs for items for her first apartment. He drew her maps of the town to help her find her way around. These maps, drawn out on napkins and old pieces of cardboard, captured the City of Village Charm in pure clarity, and they contained the firsthand knowledge of the natural wonders that only a walker could see.

But the paper plates that were once homes to donuts became the art galleries of the Corner Soda Shop. Patrons, equipment and, of course, my wife as she appeared then—young and cute, even with her mandated waitress bun on the back of her head—appeared on them. These sketches were all signed as if they were complete masterpiece canvases by the artist himself. The few that have managed to survive the more than forty years since my wife knew a member of Manchester's first family hold a special place in her heart. "Yes," I looked at my granddaughter, "your grammy knew a Cheney very well."

## Afterword

In the past few years, there has been an attempt to find some of Jake Cheney's drawings so that the historical society can preserve them. If you have any you would like to donate, the town would be grateful.

## 10

# *Fascinating Occurrences*

## D-Day Paratroopers Could Trust in Cheney Craftsmanship

This week is the seventy-fifth anniversary of D-Day, the Allied invasion of France. In the early morning hours of June 6, 1944, the skies filled with searchlights and flak, seeking the Allied planes that were preparing to drop airborne divisions. As the Allied paratroopers anxiously waited to step into the air, one remained calm and confident that his chute would carry him to the ground, unharmed.

An old story has filtered through history about this native son of Manchester. First told on the NBC radio network during the war, it appeared in the book *Unexplained Mysteries of World War II* by William Breuer. The story is of a Manchester resident among the 101st Division who is ready to liberate Europe from Nazi Germany. Robert C. Hillman was a private in the "Screaming Eagles," destined to be among the first Americans to land in France. According to the story, unlike the rest of the thousands of American jumpers that day, Hillman was not a bit anxious or even nervous about the performance of the silk parachute lifesaving device that was strapped to his back.

The Manchester resident had good cause to be confident that the silk canopy would ease his body gently to the ground hundreds of feet below the aircraft he was about to vacate. He even boastfully explained his confidence to the NBC newscaster on the outward flight from England. The silk

This silk scarf shows the Pioneer Parachute logo. *Courtesy of the Manchester Historical Society.*

parachute, he knew, had been woven, sewn and packed in his hometown. The equipment the U.S. Army had issued him was a Pioneer Parachute manufactured in Manchester, Connecticut.

The Cheney Silk Mills established Pioneer Parachute Company in 1938. It still exists today, even after several mergers, as the Pioneer Aerospace Corporation of South Windsor. Over the years, Pioneer has expanded from its humble silk canopy beginnings to test and perfect the use of nylon as well as controllable suspension lines. The company has developed the highly sophisticated devices that are still used by jumpers, airplanes and NASA spacecraft today.

In the 1940s, German paratroopers demonstrated the need for airborne troops during the invasions of Belgium and Crete. The quick-moving soldiers frustrated and devastated the traditional fighting forces of France and England. The U.S. government established its own airborne division and then added more as the war escalated.

Pioneer provided millions of parachutes to the U.S. government from 1938 onward. One such parachute, made with hometown Cheney silk, hung off Hillman's back as he prepared to drop into France.

Even more assuring to the young man was the knowledge of who had packed the chute. During the war, the massive numbers of parachutes that were needed caused manufacturers to pack them at the factory in Manchester and other factories across the nation. A tag was attached to these chutes with either the name or the initials of the packer. Another war story noted that, after bailing out of his damaged airplane, college football star Tom Harmon saved his chute and tag to track down his lifesaver. Falling in love with the young lady he discovered at the factory, he married her while she wore a dress made from the same silk. That union produced television star Mark Harmon.

Manchester's Hillman did not need to track down his packer, as he already knew her. It was his mother, Estella Hillman, who lived on Highland Street with her husband, Ronald; they were both employees of Cheney. Hillman told the newscaster that he had recognized his mother's initials on the packing tag. He was confident that his mother's handiwork would not falter that historic night.

Hillman returned to live in Manchester and work at Cheney Brothers. His tour of duty was not over, however. Like many other World War II veterans, he was called back to active duty during the Korean conflict. After returning once again to Manchester, he settled on Spruce Street before moving away again in the 1960s.

## *Afterword*

I found this description of parachute folding in the book *War Letters from Britain*, which was published in 1941. The September 1940 letter was written by Elspeth Huxley, the granddaughter-in-law of scientist Thomas Huxley. She was explaining the duties of the air force's women's auxiliary.

> *Here is another job the WAAF do—folding parachutes. It sounds easy, doesn't it—but if you had ever seen that immense quantity of fine silk material being folded into a space no larger than a sofa cushion, you wouldn't think so. There are sixty-five yards of silk in each parachute— and the hundreds of parachutes hung up in the store* [room], *incidentally, gave me a good idea of why we are going to be short of silk stockings and silk prints till the war is over. Only the very best silk can be used. There's a great art in folding a parachute, and the art lies not only in compressing all that material into the smallest possible space, but also in arranging it*

*in such a way that it will open up almost instantaneously—in one and
three-quarter seconds, to be precise—when the spring is released.*

This letter makes you realize the amazing importance of ladies such as
Estella Hillman of Manchester.

# WHEN THE INN IS THE WRONG INN

When is the inn not the inn? This was a question asked me by my
granddaughters and several people on the Pitkin Glassworks Committee.

The issue began when I was asked, "Where is the Pitkin Inn?" My
granddaughters can tell you that it is at the corner of Porter and Kensington
Streets. The sizeable purple building located there has a sign on the front,
indicating that it was the Pitkin Inn. This fact is true, but is it the inn that hosted
the dinner for French general Rochambeau on his march across Connecticut
toward the confrontation with the British at Yorktown? Yorktown is called
the last battle of the Revolutionary War—the American victory there sealed
the independence of the nation. No, that dinner took place in 1781, and the
inn facing Porter Street claims to have been constructed in the 1790s—too
late for it to have played host to the French troops.

According to several histories of the town, Richard Pitkin's wife,
Dorothy, cooked a large stew for the French troops as they passed through
Manchester, including a special dinner for their commander. Over time,
the idea that Pitkin served this meal at the Inn on Porter Street came into
maturity. It is natural for residents to connect the dinner with the inn. The
building has been included in photographs of the town for years, and it
has been included in photographs at the state historical society. The issue
is that the dates do not match. Even the sesquicentennial plague, which
was raised in 1973 near the glassworks' ruins, notes that the location of
the meal is uncertain. It reads: "Near this place stood the Pitkin Tavern
operated by Richard Pitkin and wife, Dorothy. Here, in 1775, they fed the
26 Manchester volunteers who answered the Lexington alarm. In 1781,
food was prepared by Mistress Dorothy for a part of Rochambeau's army
en route to Yorktown."

So many questions remain for us. Maybe the original inn was in the same
location and the current building replaced it. Maybe part of the original inn
can be found in the footprint of the existing structure. Perhaps the meal was

Long identified as the Pitkin Inn, this building is too new to be the inn of Revolutionary War fame. *Author's photograph.*

not served at an inn but on a property of the Pitkin family. Or maybe the dating on the building is wrong.

Of course, I have to nod to our East Hartford friends and point out that there was a Pitkin Inn in East Hartford at the time. The French commander actually spent his nights there while his army was in the area. The structure stood on Main Street near today's Silver Lane. This inn building was purchased in the 1940s and was moved out of the town.

Wherever the French troops' meal occurred, the fact remains that we don't know the truth, so the inn on Porter Street must remain the wrong Inn.

History is funny that way. It is always changing—not just in our lifetimes, but in the discovery that the beliefs we think are facts are not actually facts.


## WASHINGTON DIDN'T SLEEP HERE, BUT WE CAN PROVE HE STOPPED BY

Like in all families, there are myths and repeated stories that have survived across the generations of my family. These stories narrow in focus, teaching one point of history. Such is the case for an account of a visit from General Washington to the town of Manchester.

I explained to my granddaughter that having George Washington come to Manchester is like having a relative who played professional sports or starred in a movie. You always take great pride in pointing that fact out to someone who did not have the same story. Unlike many places across the nation that fudge the tourist catchphrase "Washington slept here," Manchester not only received a visit, but we know where and when the visit took place.

Across from the Woodbridge Barn and Farmhouse, there is a small triangle of green grass. I took my grandchildren there one day last week to show them a small stone monument. This marker, framed by flowers from the local gardening club, is one of Manchester's chief memorials and claims to fame. Inscribed in metal is a notation that President George Washington made a stop near that site at the old Woodbridge Tavern. Nearly 230 years ago (on November 9, 1789, to be exact), President Washington requested a cup of water at the tavern. He then gave the inn keeper's five-year-old daughter, Electa, a generous tip for her efforts. The event is noted in not only Woodbridge's diary but also the president's journal.

Located near the old Woodbridge Tavern, the memorial monument was erected by the author's grandfather. *Author's photograph.*

My granddaughter thought it was a great story, but then I added a little more color. I included the facts that tend to be forgotten but that make history come alive. The marker and plaque had initially been placed on the site by my granddaughter's great-great-grandfather, F. William. My father told me that he had read the same raised letters—the ones my granddaughter was touching—when they were in his father's shop on Center Street. My father also noted that the marker initially sat in a different location, but too many accidents made the town move the stone to its current position.

Not only did the young girl named Electa, receive a silver dollar from the president, but she also became the mother of seven remarkable boys. She married George Cheney, and their boys grew up to become famous artists and silk manufacturers, the very soul of the town during the late 1800s and early 1900s. Their family name still looks down from various town locations, symbolizing their importance to Manchester.

The Woodbridge Tavern visit was not Washington's first trip through Manchester. He had traveled across the town at least once, if not three other times, during the Revolutionary War. The most documented visit occurred during his journey to meet with the French commander in Lebanon, Connecticut. They planned out what was the final campaign of the American Revolution, ending with Yorktown's battle.

Besides Washington, the French legends Lafayette and General Rochambeau each visited Manchester. The young Lafayette may have also traveled through the town during the war, but he definitely visited during his 1800s grand tour of the nation. General Rochambeau came with his whole army, the same soldiers who confronted the British at Yorktown. The troops camped at various places between Lebanon and East Hartford. One evening, the French commander and his staff dined with the Pitkin family near the Pitkin Glassworks ruins. Some accounts say they dined in a tavern; others say that the meal was only prepared and served near the inn.

The building that is identified as the Pitkin Tavern on Porter Street today is not the same building the troops ate in. That building was constructed in 1790—too late to have hosted the dinner. The site of the original tavern is not known. It lies buried in the archives of Hartford's land records (Manchester was then a part of Hartford). Maybe you or my granddaughters will find the location of this first festive meal.

## MANCHESTER, WILLIMANTIC ARE LINKED BY HISTORICAL SIMILARITIES

I took one of my granddaughters to the school I work at in Willimantic. They seemed at ease, just as I had been the first time I had come to the city. It occurred to me that there is a connection between Manchester and Willimantic.

When I was working on my master's degree in education, I wrote a paper on the education systems in both Willimantic and Manchester. The two locations have several similarities. They are both small mill towns, with one company coming to dominate the economy, but still, several mills provided employment in both towns. The two cities had school fires in the same timeframe that destroyed significant buildings: Willimantic lost its high school and the normal (teacher training) school, and Manchester lost its entire Ninth District K–8 school. The makeup of the communities' residents is about the same. At first, many farming residents moved into the towns to gain employment at the mills. Then, a large number of immigrants came to work at the mills.

In general, both of the towns were typical of the mill or factory towns of the 1800s. So, why are the two towns so different today? That was the focus of my paper, and unless you are an education major looking for insight, I will not bore you with its conclusion. Instead, I will let you know how closely related the two municipalities are, which is interesting.

For example, the leading educator in Manchester history got his start in Willimantic. It helped that his mother was a well-respected teacher in the Willimantic School System. Fredrick Verplanck, the man who came to Manchester and established the high school, first taught in Willimantic. Verplanck came to Manchester at the request of the Cheney brothers, who asked him to help improve the Ninth District's educational system. He became the principal of the school, which was a K–8 school at the time, and then, he worked to establish a high school in the town. Before then, students attended Hartford Public High School to get their high school degrees.

Verplanck also witnessed the devastating fire of the large school complex on Main Street (1913), the construction of its replacement (Bennet Academy) and the hiring of the school's staff.

Other achievements that Verplanck brought to Manchester included a teacher training facility associated with the New Britain Normal School (later called the Central Connecticut State University). He facilitated the construction of the old high school on Main Street (1910) and the consolidation of all the town's independent education districts into one public school union.

Malcolm Stannard, the longtime editor of the *Willimantic Chronicle* and *Hartford Times*, cut his teeth in the news business at the *Manchester Evening Herald*. He even helped start my writing career at the *Chronicle*.

Another connection between the two towns came in the workers at the mills. Connecticut's first silk mill was located in Willimantic. Its skilled workers and workers from other Willimantic mills found employment at the Cheney Silk Mills.

There is one story of the Cheney Brothers sneaking into the other town to steal a supervisor. It seems that a Willimantic mill had a foreman the Cheney's wanted in Manchester. Because he lived in a company house, the foreman could not announce he was leaving, as his family would have been thrown out into the cold. So, after dark one day, one of the founding seven Cheney brothers appeared outside the foreman's house with a couple of wagons and a hired hand. The men and women quickly loaded the carts with the family's belongings and scurried away into the night. The next day, the foreman appeared at the Manchester mills in his new position, and his family busied themselves with arranging their new home in town.

## *Afterword*

There is a small error in this column. The first silk mill in Connecticut was actually located in Mansfield, the town next to Willimantic. A fellow history columnist noticed this issue but added that Willimantic did have silk mills operating in the town while Cheney Brothers were first starting. He felt that the foreman story was possible.

# FLOOD

*Flood*—the word brings to mind the shore of the Connecticut River. Yearly, we read of the flooding at these places, with images of rising water swallowing buildings and homes.

As a reporter in Glastonbury, I wrote about the efforts of the Main Street merchants to sandbag their shops, knowing that if the sandbags worked, the insurance companies would cover their costs. If flooding did occur, then the merchants had to eat the money spent on sandbags and settle for designated money written in their policies.

Hop Brook is tamed today, but in 1869, it was not. *Author's photograph.*

Manchester, located ten miles away from the Connecticut River, never appeared to be a flood area to me. But there was a flood here on October 9, 1869, which devastated commercial ventures of the town, creating a new face for Manchester, a look that we still wear today.

After a summer of little precipitation, the area was inundated with rain for about a week before October 9. This rain swelled the area lakes and small ponds until the dams could not withstand the pressure. According to records, every factory dam but one in Manchester failed during this flood. That is not a fantastic fact when looking around town today. But in 1869, the Hop and Porter Brooks alone had eighteen mill dams. These dams provided waterpower for mills, many of these paper or paper product producers.

Manchester had one of the oldest paper mills in the state, which dated back to the 1700s. Manchester paper was used by the *Hartford Courant* the day it printed about the Battle of Lexington. The town was a center for paper production in Connecticut. Manchester's own Bunce family pioneered and trained later generations in paper production.

On October 9, as each dam failed, increasing debris and water pounded on the next barrier and mill site. The ever-growing avalanche of destruction inundated mill after mill as it swept downhill from Case Mountain, toward the level area near East Hartford. The wave ended by destroying the Lewis Bunce and Sons Paper complex near the town line beyond recovery. Other paper mills, such as the Henry E. Roger's Mill and other Bunce family mills, were severely damaged, and many ceased operations in town. The Cheney Brothers Silk Mill on Hop Brook was damaged but rose again like the legendary phoenix, giving the south end of town a new industrial focus.

In the North End, the flood destroyed all the dams from Talcottville to the railroad station on North Main Street. The only dam left standing was the one at Union Pond. This structure, which had been newly rebuilt in 1866 by the Union Manufacturing Company, withstood the flooding along the Hockanum River. The Union Manufacturing Company was a textile mill, too.

Historian William Buckley recalled that not a single death was related to the flooding, but there were harrowing near-disastrous events. The raging waters forced a worker who was checking the Union Pond dam to climb a nearby tree to escape. He remained there overnight before he could be safely rescued. The Hockanum River swept away a four-family home in Union Village before damaging the factories downstream and washing away the road bridges at Union Street and North Main.

The town was almost isolated from the rest of the state during the flooding as well. The waters had destroyed a culvert at Parker Village, blocking the railroad tracks and downing the telegraph wires. No trains were running in or out of town. The only road open out of town ran from the Green to Bolton. Most of the town's bridges had disappeared along with the dams.

Buckley concluded his article with a glimmer of luck, "Bad as the destruction seemed, it would probably have been worse had the dam at Snenipsit Lake in Rockville gave way." A previous historian wrote that, by the time the October 1869 afternoon was over, Manchester had affectively said goodbye to its paper industry. The textile mills remained, and first the Union Mill, and then the Cheney Mill led the town into prosperity.

# BOTH SLAVERY AND UNDERGROUND RAILROAD ARE PART OF MANCHESTER HISTORY

"Grandpa, were there slaves in Manchester?" my granddaughter asked, as her school has been looking into the four hundredth anniversary of the first slave ships coming to what became the United States. I had to answer yes. Many people only think of slavery happening in the southern states, but in reality, slavery was an accepted practice in most of the northern states until the 1840s.

Connecticut officially banned slavery in 1848. Initially, the rule only freed the children who were born to enslaved people after that time. The others had to be released by their owners. Mathias Spiess's 1923 town

This stone house is on Connecticut's Freedom Trail, and it is one of the few remaining structures that was built by freeman Alpheus Quincy. *Author's photograph.*

history explained that a section of Manchester was set aside to cover the cost of feeding and sheltering an old slave named Flo, whose owner had neglected her care. The book stated, "Located somewhere within the town limits of Manchester are two hundred acres of land [probably on Middle Turnpike between Main and Adams Street], which was 'set off for the support of Old Flo,' a female negro slave owned by Elisha P. Pitkin until his death [on] August 1, 1819."

Flo was born in the year 1752 and lived to be so old that Pitkin forgot or neglected to support her. In October 1830, Piktin's estate executors were summoned by the town to reimburse the community for the support this woman had received from. The law required the Pitkins to care for Old Flo during her lifetime. The income of the two hundred acres was to be used to cover the expenses of her boarding, clothes and other needs. She spent her last years "at Warren's house" near Silver Lane.

Besides Old Flo, town records show that Pitkin also owned Flo's five children, who were born into slavery, and another female slave named Gin. This enslaved woman also had a daughter named Dinah. The census of 1790 showed that thirty-one enslaved people lived in the town of East

Hartford, which included Manchester. Spiess also wrote that the Podunk Natives of Manchester were captured and sold into slavery.

Besides the enslaved people who were owned in the town, other slaves traveled through our community. Many of these slaves were escaping toward Canada. Manchester was a stop on the Underground Railroad. The Connecticut Freedom Trail notes that the Hart Porter House, which is still standing on Porter Street, was used as a safe haven for escaping slaves. The outbuildings located on the property have a hidden room that can be reached by a secret doorway. Porter was a member of the Methodist church, which supported the abolitionist movement. The church even brought famed ex-slave Fredrick Douglass to town in 1843 to speak against slavery.

Another Manchester site mentioned on the Freedom Trail is the Walter Bunce House on Bidwell Street. Alpheus Quincy, a freeman, constructed this large stone home. The information presented states that Quincy built similar fieldstone buildings around the area. This house is one of the few of these dwellings that is still standing.

# REMEMBERING THOSE WHO SERVED IN KOREA AS VETERANS DAY APPROACHES

With Veterans Day on people's minds, my granddaughter looked at me and asked, "Do you know a veteran?" I smiled. I know many veterans; some who eagerly joined, some who waited for the pull of the draft and many you would never know were veterans. "Great-Grandpa was a veteran. He was the typical veteran." She looked confused, and I explained.

In June 1950, the North Koreans came over the hills and mountains of the Korean Peninsula, driving the South Korean army into a panicked flight. The American commander in Japan, General Douglas McArthur, ordered a small detachment of American troops into the peninsula to help stem the flow of the North Koreans. The small force was actually told that their uniforms would be enough firepower against the aggressor and that they would be able to stop the advance with little effort.

That proved to be wrong, however, so MacArthur sent a larger detachment, then a whole division, then a second division and so on. The North Koreans drove on headlong, unstoppable even against the Americans, until they pushed the defenders into the Pusan Perimeter at the bottom of the peninsula. Later, MacArthur engineered a breakout by landing troops behind the North Korean lines at Inchon. At the same time, General Walton Walker, "Johnnie Walker," led a breakout operation from Pusan northward to link up with the new invading army.

What does this have to do with my father? He served in Korea—for less than a year—but he served and even went over the side of the boat at Inchon. How did this man who was nearly unfit for service end up in Korea? Well, a few years earlier, in 1948, the country had launched a peacetime draft. My father and his friends from town tried to enlist in the Connecticut National Guard. The healthy Manchester boys were welcomed with open arms, becoming part-time soldiers in the guard, bypassing the requirement of being drafted into the regular army. My father, who had flat feet, a bad heart and an easily dislocated shoulder, was declared unfit. He watched as his friends spent their weekends in olive drab, and he continued his work as a teller in a bank.

Once the Korean conflict erupted, President Truman declared a national draft of men between the ages of eighteen and forty-five. My father breathed a little easy—he figured he would be declared 4-F (unfit for service) and would not have to serve if he was drafted. However, he was not; the draft board doctor gave him three Ds and an F, and my father was a soldier. There was no debating or asking another doctor to find a reason for him to remain a civilian, only a sense of duty to his country. By the end of 1950, he was inducted into the U.S. Army and served in New Jersey as a mail clerk. From there, with less than a year left in his service time, he was sent to Korea. It was an experience he hardly talked about.

What about those smart Manchester boys who joined the national guard? Well, President Truman nationalized the guard when he saw he needed additional troops because of Korea. They were issued weapons and placed on a transport to Germany, where they sat out the threat posed by the communists in North Korea.

## Afterword

I attended the history center's Veteran Talk. It gave me a chance to gather with the men I admired as a boy—the same men who instilled the pride in me that caused me to volunteer for the service. I even got a chance to say thank you in person.

# SNOW DAYS ARE FACTS OF CHILDHOOD, BUT THEY'RE NOT THE REASON FOR TOWN'S MOST FAMOUS SCHOOL CLOSING

It is winter, and my granddaughters watch the TV, looking for the name of their town in hope and anticipation. A snow day is a delight that we all recall from our school days. As a young boy, I would listen to WTIC 1080's Bob Steele to see if I had to venture through the snow. My father could not recall how he learned of snow days, but it was most likely by the radio.

Schools are closed—now and before—for reasons other than just snow. A few years back, it was a fall hurricane that also canceled Halloween. When my father was a small boy, it was a 1938 hurricane that blew through town, closing schools.

One of the most memorable school closings I lived through took place when I was a senior at Manchester High School. One day, just after I arrived, the school was closed because there was no electricity. What made it so great was that, minutes after the doors flew open and the students cascaded out of the building, the power came back on, but of course, it was too late to call all of us back.

I also remember a weeklong closure that occurred because of an ice storm in the early 1970s. The Manchester newspapers recalled another week that was lost to the Spanish influenza in 1918. Too many of the teachers were sick.

To me, the most unusual Manchester school closing did not come about because of the weather. The day was pristine. It was not electrical, water or even heating problems that closed the schools; all of the buildings were in perfect working order. It was not a bomb scare, which happened when I was young. No, there was no danger to students or teachers anywhere. The most respected superintendent of schools—not only here in Manchester, but across the state—called the day, so it was not a mistake.

According to an article in the local newspaper from 1938, a simple phone call at 2:53 a.m. on Monday, November 11, 1918, caused the town of Manchester to go nuts. This call caused police officers to race in all directions from Main Street to either turn on the streetlights (at the time, they were turned off at 11:00 p.m. each night) or to blare factory whistles and ring church bells. The noise roused sleeping residents throughout Manchester, bringing them into the streets. The weather was chilly but calm. Most of the people who were there a hundred years ago did not think about the weather at all. They were too excited, too full of joy. It seemed that the war, the First World War, had ended and that the prisoners of war had been released immediately.

Town fathers, among them Frank Cheney Jr. and the ever-unflappable superintendent of schools Frederick Verplanck, gathered on Main Street. Cheers and cries from the gathered residents echoed off the surrounding brick buildings. Members of the Salvation Army Band arrived, instruments in hand, and struck up a martial tune. The music set feet stomping, and the crowd gathered in improvised companies, forming a battalion of marching feet. From one end of Main Street to the other, the marching human wave undulated, bringing with it joy and laughter. Joining with the band were other noise-making instruments. The paper's account states that Cheney played two garbage can lids as he marched along the route. The spontaneous celebration continued for hours in the glow of streetlights, house lights and under the blare of every mill whistle and church bell found in the town.

At about 3:30 a.m., red-faced with excitement, Cheney instructed his foreman that no steam needed to be run up for the factory, as there would be no work at the mill that day. The equally joyous Frank Verplanck declared that the schools would be closed that day.

## Recent Revelations Place Town's First Movie Theater on Main Street

"Did you go to the movies when you were little?" my granddaughter asked the other day as the film with *Frozen* characters finished scrolling across the screen. "Yes, but there was only one movie at a time to pick for each of the theaters," I smiled back. That was not the actual truth, but it allowed my granddaughter to understand that the multiscreen theater is a newer situation.

Looking back at Manchester history, you find that there have been several movie theaters in the town. The oldest one has been a debated historical society topic for many years, that is until the past few months, when long lost photographic evidence has finally appeared.

From the Old State Theater on Main Street to the UA theaters at the Parkade, my knowledge of the "professional" theater is limited. I know that there had been a theater on Oak Street called the Circle Theatre. It dated from 1913, when the temporary home of the House Department Store was converted to show silent films. This building was redecorated in the mid-1910s and then entirely replaced by the 1920s to allow for the running of sound films. The new building, called the New Circle Theatre, took up the back end of the House and Hale building. But the Circle was not the oldest movie theater either.

In the early 1900s, the Apel Opera House in the North End showed movies every now and again, but it was not exclusively a film theater. No, the first such theater was located on Main Street, about midway down from Center Congregational Church. It was in a building that also hosted the American Hotel. This theater was called the Edison, the Imperial and the Globe as time went on. It dated back to the late 1800s, with the invention of the Edison nickelodeon.

The historical society had a picture of this facility but could not say for sure that it was the first theater in town. That changed when a visitor to the Old Manchester Museum came in with a copy of her grandfather's history. This grandfather, Paul Housmann, had been a member of the South Manchester Volunteer Fire Department and was stationed at what is now Bennet Academy. Housmann was a responder to a 1908 Main Street fire, where he took a remarkable picture of a destroyed American Hotel building that was once located next to the Weldon building. This fire occurred on December 28, 1908, and was mentioned in a *Hartford Courant* article at the time. A copy of this article notes that the fire started in the Imperial Movie Theater, clearly placing the Edison as the oldest establishment that was dedicated to just movie projection. The cause of the fire was not listed, but the write up assumed it had started in the theater. Could it have been an overheated projector that ignited the flammable film of the time?

What town records indicate is that the Edison Theater was once fined by Manchester officials for showing movies on a Sunday. In the early silent film era, there was a movement among the residents to prevent films from being offered during holidays and on the Sabbath. Imagine what Hollywood's response would have been if it could not have Christmas releases?

Prior to the COVID-19 pandemic, the historical society offered movies for viewing on Thursday nights. The organization advertised these events by using the old photograph of the Edison. So, the first movie theater is once again calling in viewers.

## GRAIN OF SALT: ACTORS

The draw of the footlights affects the visions of many young residents of Manchester, from the actors of the Little Theater of Manchester to the players of the stage at Manchester High School and East Catholic High School. Over the years, countless students and adults have dreamed of the life as a matinee star or more serious Broadway, opera and musical fame. Manchester has not been immune to the entertainment bug, but who can we set as models for our children?

Horace Cheney frowned at the thought that his son would have succumbed to the acting bug's bite, but now, we, as a society, would have looked on with hope and encouragement. My grandfather was a cornet player in the Manchester German American Band; his oldest son went on to play with the big bands of the 1930s and 1940s. My aunt followed the music bug to New York but ended up teaching music in Irvington, New Jersey, for forty years. Other want-to-be residents have set out on the road, only to fall victim to the saying, "So many have great talent, but few have the luck to be the one." It is that way in the business of entrainment. Incredibly talented people surround you, and it comes down to the lucky one. One of the lucky ones came from Manchester.

Growing up in Manchester, I never knew the name of that lucky one, but I remembered the face from the flickering screen of my parents' TV—yes, originally in black and white and then in color. The face I recalled was in black and white, but it didn't have to be. Born in South Manchester around the same time as my aunt, this woman grew up to shine down from the motion picture palaces of the 1930s and 1940s. Astrid Allwyn was her acting name. OK, you may not know that name. She appeared in over twenty films, including three Academy Award Best Picture nominees and one of the most famous motion pictures of all time.

Because of her foreign-sounding name, Hollywood agents pitched Astrid as a Swedish beauty, similar to the model Greta Garbo. But she was born in Manchester in 1905, the daughter of Ernest and Albertina Christofferson. Astrid followed her call to the stage and then to the movies. By the 1930s, she had solidified her position in the industry as the rival love interest character, but she rarely achieved the star-level character. She did play opposite of some of the top talents of the time, including Shirley Temple, Humphrey Bogart, James Stewart, Irene Dunne and Loretta Young. She also appeared in the most-demanded film of the 1940s—*Mr. Smith Goes to Washington*. This film, pitting a small-town senator against a corrupt political machine, was the most requested film throughout Europe after the occupying Nazi governments announced one last importation of Hollywood films.

An interesting fact about Astrid is that she left the screen when she was a young lady to raise her children. This retirement ended her appearance in movies in the early 1940s. One wonders if there had been a demand for older women to dominate the screen if Astrid would have made a comeback. But we can always enjoy her talent. Every time you watch *Mr. Smith Goes to Washington*, remember that Susan, the daughter of Senator Paine, came from Manchester.

## Town Elections of the Past Included Many Socialist Candidates

"Grandpa, what's a Republican or Democrat?" My granddaughter's question came after hearing a political advertisement on TV. During election years, political advertisements appear on air and on our lawns. These two political parties dominate our attention now, but that was not always the case.

Back in the early 1900s, Manchester had active Socialist, Progressive and Prohibitionist Parties that were separate from the national Republican and Democratic Parties. Although Manchester had been a staunch Republican town from the Civil War to the 1950s, the people elected a socialist to be selectman. A quick research of records at the town hall reveals that Selectman William Schieldge represented the Socialist Party. A well-respected businessman in town, Schieldge's name appeared consistently throughout the early 1900s as a socialist candidate for the positions of selectman and a representative in the Connecticut General Assembly. He was elected selectman in 1912 and served several terms on that board and in other town offices.

But Schieldge was not be the only socialist candidate that would be synonymous with Manchester history. Other leading citizens would support the party's platform, calling for women's education and voting rights, improved working conditions and more government control of big business. The party also served as a choice for young voters who did not want to follow in their parents' political footsteps.

Businessman Mathew Moriarty and town historian Mathis Spiess ran on the Socialist Party ticket. Moriarty ran for selectman in 1918 and 1920, and he ran for a position in the general assembly in 1910. Spiess ran on the Socialist Party ticket for state assembly in 1916. The records also indicate that another multiyear candidate ran for public office in Manchester. This Manchester citizen sent his two daughters to Connecticut College in the 1920s and saw them graduate when most young women at the time barely

F.W. Kanehl with his family. He looks more mature in this picture, which was taken during the time he was running for selectman as a socialist. *Author's collection.*

made it out of high school. He also allowed his children to be artists and musicians instead of following in his field of endeavor, construction. This man, F. William Kanehl, was my grandfather.

Oh, did I just feel my Republican father roll over in his grave?

Town and state records, as well as local newspaper archives, opened my eyes to this political reality. I knew that my grandfather had been instrumental in the building of Manchester—quite literally—as he was a general contractor. His efforts included the construction of commercial buildings, churches and various residential housing developments from the early 1900s until his death in 1958. But amazingly, I discovered that my grandfather, the person my father said "never did anything in the community other than work," actually ran for selectman three times, from 1918 to 1920. He even ran for a position in the general assembly in 1920 and 1922. To be fair, my grandfather participated in these political ventures before my father was born.

It seems that my grandfather had an active social life in the early 1900s, being a member of the German American Band and participating in various discussion groups of the time. This social life led to his involvement in the small but vocal Socialist Party. The Manchester Socialist Party participated in town elections from the early 1900s until the Great Depression. The other smaller parties came and went as the issues of the day dictated. My "quiet" grandfather did muster over 150 votes for the position in the general assembly in 1920.

Why my grandfather stopped his apparent involvement in the political arena, I cannot say. The end of his socialistic career coincided with the Great Depression. This financial nightmare not only changed how people survived, but also how the political machines operated. The Socialist Party changed its approach and vision during this era, becoming more interested in a class revolt than just reform. This was most likely why some of the top names in Manchester history faded from its ranks.

## Afterword

Like most immigrants to this nation, my grandfather's family came over from Europe with a desire for change. Again, like most immigrants to Manchester, he arrived at the harbor (in his case, Boston, not New York) and saw a man holding a sign that said, "Hiring Cheney Brothers—Manchester, Connecticut." There were many other companies on the site with the same hiring method. Why he choose Manchester, we will never know.

Starting as a stonemason and bricklayer in town, he grew his carpentry and building business to great success. A progressive for his time, he always told my father that his children could be what they wanted to be and do what they wanted to do—not just construction. However, he did make his two boys learn the trades, just in case.

He also felt that boys and girls were equal, which was why both my aunts attended Connecticut College for Women. Both had successful careers, one as an artist and the other as a musician and teacher.

After the Great Depression, my grandfather continued to work. My father was born in 1928. He only remembered the steady "work-every-day" F. William Kanehl. He had no clue of the young man who allowed his name to be associated with the liberal progressives of the town.

# 11

# *Other Columns*

## THE LUTZ BEAR: GONE BUT NOT FORGOTTEN FROM HISTORY BUILDING ON CEDAR STREET

When people of a certain age walk into the Old Manchester Museum, they sometimes get a funny smile on their faces. Looking straight ahead as they come through the door, they expect to see—and often do in their imaginations—the bear.

For decades, a giant stuffed bear, standing upright on its hind legs, greeted people who came through that doorway. It was the welcoming host of the Lutz Junior Museum, which occupied the Cedar Street building until 1982. My grandchildren and their grandmother wanted to know the history of the bear.

The bear is still welcoming children of all ages at the Lutz Children's Museum, now located on South Main Street in the Old South School. My grandchildren have each been frightened and amazed by the generous gift of William Sleith. According to the accompanying plaque, the Manchester resident "took" the bear in 1966 while visiting Kodiak Island in Alaska. The Alaska brown bear (*Ursus middendorffi*) still brings smiles to the faces of my granddaughters' grandmother as well. Memories filled with rock collections and scientific facts are being shared from one generation to another at the children's museum.

This Klondike bear was the longtime greeter at the Lutz Museum. *Author's photograph.*

The Lutz Junior Museum was the brainchild of longtime Manchester Public School art teacher Hazel P. Lutz. She started the museum by arranging and cataloging the materials town residents donated to the cause of children's education. This collection was initially displayed and offered to schools in kits from the basement of the Waddell School. The artifacts eventually moved to the Cedar Street building in 1958. For most of the next three decades, the museum was open for people to come enjoy the collection and take classes in science and art. Today, the basement of the Cedar Street building still has the classrooms set aside in the hope that, one day, it can offer history-oriented education to the children of Manchester.

Besides the museum building, the organization runs the outdoor class experience at Oak Grove Nature Center. This fifty-three-acre site was presented to the organization by the town in 1964 and has provided countless children and adults with authentic nature studies as they travel along the site's many trails.

Before the science museum occupied the current home of the history museum, it was the kindergarten space for the Washington School children. One visitor noted that building had two kindergarten classes on its two sides and provided the children with an excellent education separate from the rest of the Washington School population.

Before it housed the Washington School, the building was a school for the Cheney Silk Mill workers and the Cheney children themselves. The building, constructed in 1859, was initially situated on a different corner of the property. It featured two doors for the children to enter, one for the boys and one for the girls. Families of the original mill-operating brothers and members of the second generation sent their children there before sending them off to complete their high school educations in Hartford. Today, you can still walk through the same doors that these giants of the American silk industry used as children. You can picture the bear greeting you as it had for the earlier generations of Manchester residents when they were young.


# HISTORY BEHIND HIGH SCHOOL MASCOT IS RELATIVELY RECENT

It stands just under eight feet tall and stares at you with its one eye. My granddaughter stood in front of the plywood cut-out, staring back. "Why is it here?" she naturally asked.

"My father collected everything," I said, meaning that he refused to throw anything away.

"But why are there two?"

"There was one for each side of the Sesquicentennial parade float."

The Indian heads initially dominated the sides of the float, representing the high school as it ventured down Main Street in 1973. Their freshly painted faces stared out at the crowd as their still-attached feathers fluttered in the breeze. Now, the two Manchester High School mascots block the windows at my father's barn, where they came to rest after their moment in the sun.

"Is that what you wore when you were in high school?"

"No," I answered, and I explained and recalled that Manchester High School was the home of the Indians. It is a mascot name that I remember from when I was a student forty years ago. I

In 1973, this Native American represented the local high school. Today, the mascot has been changed. *Author's photograph.*

know that there was a time when new mascot names—more in line with the history of the town—were being considered, like the Silkworms. Unlike the sports fans of East Hampton, who took their nickname, the Bellringers, from the bell factories that dominated the economy in that town, our silken past did not catch on.

The name Indians still rings through the halls and across the playing fields and courts, but Manchester's mascot was not always the Indians. My father, who graduated in 1945, was not an "Indian" when he represented the school. No, he was a Red Man. From its time on Main Street to now, on Middle Turnpike, the team colors of the high school have always been red and white. So, the sports teams and the other teams that represented Manchester were known by the nickname Reds or Red Men. That nickname, you would think, may have morphed into the Indians of modern times.

Dave Smith, the curator of the Old Manchester Museum, and I researched this question. We discovered that "Indians" became the nickname only in 1949, after it was presented to the faculty and student body. Smith explained that he had recently received a question from several students at Manchester High School about the origin of the high school's Indian mascot. After some research through the historical society's collection of Manchester's *High School World*, we discovered that the first mention of Indians connected with the high school was in the December 8, 1949 issue of the *High School World*. The article began: "Heap big change, you betchum! Manchester High School has decided to call itself the Indians." This name was decided on by the student body, which wanted to have a mascot. The cheerleaders introduced new cheers at an assembly of the students. The article went on to say that the students' response to the nickname proved enthusiastic.

The *High School World* was a student publication that ran in the local *Manchester Evening Herald*. The local newspaper devoted one full page each week to Manchester High School news and happenings. Beginning in September 1933, the publication continued until May 1989, a run of more than fifty-five years. The museum has a vast collection of these pages, as well as Manchester High School's yearbooks. Its archives provide researchers a glimpse into the mind's eye of generations of the town's teenagers. Usually, when adults write history, these primary sources can provide a refreshing point of view.

## *Afterword*

Shortly after this column appeared, a group of Manchester High School students petitioned the school board, requesting a new mascot name. After an uproar by older residents and counterarguments by the students, the board agreed to change the mascot to Red Hawks.

## Nativity Scene Has Long History and Several Homes in Manchester

As you travel through what most people call the center of Manchester during the holiday season, you are greeted by friendly fiberglass faces. These human and animal faces have welcomed visitors from the First Congregational Church's grassy side yard since the 1980s. But they are much older than the forty years they have weathered through the Connecticut holiday seasons at that site.

Each year, the town of Manchester places its manger scene alongside Center Congregational Church. This scene has been part of the city for longer than anyone can remember. The town's parks department cannot answer the simple questions of when and how the town acquired the Nativity scene. No one in the department has been employed long enough to know. Even a promised look through the historical files did not help.

Nate Agostinelli, who served as mayor in the 1970s, noted that "it seemed to have always been part of the town." Like my father, he remembered it being set up each year in Center Memorial Park, just below the Mary Cheney Library building. "Ruining the sledding," as my father and others remembered.

This yearly occurrence happened from the 1940s to the late 1970s. Each year, the figures were hauled out of storage and positioned in front of a wooden stable that was generally constructed by students of Howell Cheney Technical School from materials donated by local businesses.

The archives of the Old Manchester Museum brought forward two newspaper articles on the 1979 display—one of the last placements of the scene alongside the library. These articles noted that the fiberglass figures were purchased in 1969 to replace other figures that were deteriorating—not to mention that no one knew what these other figures were constructed of or whom they were constructed by. The 1969 figures were presented to the town by a fundraising organization composed of town fraternal- and community-oriented groups. This Nativity scene committee was spearheaded by the local branch of the Tall Cedars of Lebanon. The committee raised nearly $4,500 to continue the holiday tradition. Over four hundred residents gathered in Center Park on November 30, 1969, to unveil the new twenty-piece fiberglass display.

A smaller Nativity scene, which was purchased at the same time, was also erected yearly in the north end of Manchester in the 1970s. Its location, after the completion of the region's redevelopment, was at the intersection of Main and North Main Streets.

Every year, this Nativity scene greets travelers to central Manchester. *Author's photograph.*

One article added the fact that the library had been the larger Nativity scene's location for twenty-two years, which would place the original figures as being residents of town since 1946. The larger Nativity was moved its current holiday location due to concerns expressed in the late 1970s about the town placing a religious display on town-owned land.

The question remains, however, when did the original scene come to the town? Does anyone out there know if the larger manger scene was ever located anywhere other than in Center Memorial Park and at the Congregational church?

In the 1930s, a large tree near St. James Church was used by the town for its annual tree-lighting ceremony. Was the manger purchased initially or donated to go alongside the tree? A 1938 hurricane took down that "Christmas" tree along with St. James's steeple, and the tree-lighting ceremony ended.

So many questions remain. Can anyone shed some light? Besides the age of the original manger scene, whatever happened to the smaller Nativity? What other town holiday traditions have either disappeared or been replaced?

# Bibliography

## Primary Sources

Archives of the *Hartford Courant*

Archives of the Library of Congress. Legion of Merit, 1918, Distinguished Service Medal. Washington, D.C.

Archives of the *Manchester Evening Herald*

Archives of the Manchester Historical Society. Manchester, CT.

Archives of the Windsor Historical Society. Windsor, CT.

Brown, Wilson. "Aide to Four Presidents." *American Heritage Magazine*, February 1955.

Cheney, Margreta Swenson. *If All the Great Men—The Cheneys of Manchester.* Manchester, CT: Cheney Homestead, 1975.

Forbes-Robertson, Diana, et al. *War Letters from Britain.* New York: G.P. Putnam's Sons, 1941.

Kilpatrick, Archie. *World War II History of Manchester, Connecticut.* New York: Hobson Book Press, 1946.

McCoy, Frank. "Memorial Biography of Sherwood Cheney, by Frank McCoy (Fellow Classmate) for Assembly." *West Point Alumni Magazine*, July 1950.

## Secondary Sources

Anonymous. *Organization of the American Expeditionary Forces*. Vol. 1. Reprint, Washington, D.C.: Center of Military History, United States Army, 1988.

Breuer, William B. "Parachute in a Million." In *Unexplained Mysteries of World War II*. Edison, NJ: Chartwell Books, 2016, 72–73.

Buckley, William. *New England Pattern: The History of Manchester, Connecticut*. Chester, CT: Pequot Press, 1973.

Lewis, Thomas R. *Silk Along Steel: The Story of the South Manchester Railroad*. Manchester, CT: Manchester Community College Press, 1976.

Spiess, Mathias. *The History of Manchester, Connecticut*. Manchester, CT: Centennial Committee of the Town of Manchester, 1924.

Weaver, Glenn, and Michael Swift. *Hartford, Connecticut's Capital: An Illustrated History*. Sun Valley, CA: American History Press, 2003.

Williams, Alice Farley. *Silk & Guns: The Life of a Connecticut Yankee, Frank Cheney, 1817–1904*. Manchester, CT: Manchester Historical Society, 1996.

# About the Author

A longtime newspaper reporter and teacher, Robert Kanehl has had a lifelong interest in history. This love of history has appeared in his classroom teaching as well as his writing. He has over thirty years of teaching experience in both Maine and Connecticut. Aside from this book, Mr. Kanehl is the author of several young adult historical novels, including *Murder in the Newsroom*, *Hannah's Ghost* and *Facing the Fire*.

Mr. Kanehl is a member of the Manchester Historical Society, serving as the town's museum guide and formally serving on the society's board of directors. He is the secretary of the Pitkin Glass Works executive board and writes a "History of Manchester" column for the *Journal Inquirer* newspaper.

Robert Kanehl currently lives with his wife in Manchester, Connecticut.